Transatlantic relations in the prospect of an enlarged European Community

by Theodore Geiger

Chief of International Studies,
National Planning Association
Washington D.C.

BRITISH-NORTH AMERICAN COMMITTEE

Sponsored by
British-North American Research Association
National Planning Association (U.S.A.)
Private Planning Association of Canada

SBN 902594 01 X
Library of Congress Catalog Card Number 75-141647

Published by the British-North American Committee
Printed and bound in Great Britain by Alfred H. Cooper & Sons Ltd, London

November 1970

Contents

The British-North American Committee

At the Committee's first meeting in New York City, December 1969, the following statement of its aims was authorised:

The British-North American Committee has been established to study and comment upon the developing relationships between Britain, the United States and Canada. It seeks to promote clearer understanding of the economic opportunities and problems facing the three countries, to explore areas of co-operation and of possible friction and to discover constructive responses. It believes that sound relations between these three countries in the context of an increasingly interrelated world are essential to future prosperity and seeks to promote better understanding through the collection of facts and their widespread dissemination.

In serving these aims, the Committee is sponsoring a series of objective studies undertaken by qualified experts in the three countries and published with the Committee's approval. On the basis of these factual studies and of discussions at its meeting, the Committee may also issue policy statements signed by its members.

The Committee's membership – listed on pp. xv-xvii – includes business, labour, agricultural, and professional leaders from Britain, the United States, and Canada. The Committee is sponsored by three non-profit research organisations — the British-North American Research Association in London, the National Planning Association in Washington, and the Private Planning Association in Montreal, described on pp. xviii & xix.

The British-North American Committee is a unique organisation both in terms of its broadly diversified membership and in terms of its blending of factual studies and policy conclusions on British-North American relations. It meets twice a year, once in Great Britain and once in North America. Its work is jointly financed by funds contributed from private sources in Canada, Great Britain and in the United States.

Offices on behalf of the Committee are maintained at 1606 New Hampshire Avenue, NW, Washington, DC 20009, and at 12 Upper Belgrave Street, London, SW1. George Goyder serves as British Secretary of the Committee and John Miller (Assistant Chairman and Executive Secretary of the National Planning Association) serves as North American Secretary. Simon Webley in London and Sperry Lea in Washington are the Co-Directors of Research.

Howick — Harold W Sweatt

LORD HOWICK — HAROLD SWEATT

Co-Chairmen of the Committee

Statement of the British-North American Committee
to accompany the Report

In view of its concern with transatlantic relationships, the British-North American Committee, as one of its first actions, requested an analysis of the probable course of developments affecting the Atlantic region, assuming that the European Community is enlarged by the addition of the United Kingdom and other European countries.

This study has been undertaken by Dr. Theodore Geiger, Chief of International Studies of the National Planning Association in Washington, and was presented in draft form to the Committee at its meeting at Farnham Castle, England, on June 26th-28th, 1970.

Dr. Geiger describes the prospects for the Atlantic region and the history of European and Atlantic integration up to the present day. He then discusses the major factors and trends which are likely to shape their future development, and the possible responses by the Atlantic nations, particularly the United States.

Dr. Geiger's analysis and conclusions are his own. Without necessarily endorsing them, the British-North American Committee recommends publication of this study in the belief that it makes a significant and timely contribution to the understanding of important issues affecting Britain, Canada and the United States.

Members of the Committee signing the statement

Co-Chairmen:

LORD HOWICK
Chairman, Commonwealth Development Corporation

HAROLD SWEATT
Honorary Chairman of the Board, Honeywell Inc.

Chairman, Executive Committee

ROBERT M. FOWLER
President, Canadian Pulp and Paper Association

Members

A. E. BALLOCH
President, Bowater's Canadian Corporation Ltd

DAVID BARRAN
Chairman, Shell Transport and Trading Company Ltd

LEONARD BEATON
London

PETER BESSELL
London

JAMES H. BINGER
Chairman of the Board, Honeywell Inc.

WILLIAM S. BREWSTER
Chairman of the Board, USM Corporation

HARRY BRIDGES
President, Shell Canada Ltd

LLEWELLYN L. CALLAWAY, JR.
Vice-Chairman, *Newsweek*, Inc.

DR. CHARLES CARTER
Vice-Chancellor, University of Lancaster

H. F. R. CATHERWOOD
Director-General, National Economic Development Council

FRANCOIS E. CLEYN
Chairman of the Board and Chief Executive Officer, Cleyn & Tinker Ltd

HON. J. V. CLYNE
Chairman and Chief Executive Officer, MacMillan Bloedel Ltd

Transatlantic relations in the prospect of an enlarged European Community

by Theodore Geiger

Author's Preface

The prospect that the European Community may soon be enlarged by the addition, as full or associate members, of the United Kingdom and other European countries provides both the need and the opportunity to examine the implications of such a development for transatlantic relationships. A change of this magnitude in the nature of the European Community is bound to affect its future evolution in significant ways. And, the probable development of the European Community in the years to come will be a very important, if not the main, influence on the future relationships between Western Europe and North America — that is, on the character of the Atlantic region as a whole.

A valid assessment of the nature and relative probabilities of the various possible courses of development in Western Europe and the Atlantic region cannot be made in the perspective solely of today's relationships and of current interests and problems. It is possible to project the future only on the basis of long-term continuing trends and of analysis of how they are likely to be modified both by deliberate human decisions and actions and by the ongoing momentum of the institutions, values and norms of behavior of the societies and cultures concerned.

Accordingly, this report sketches the development since World War II of the main structural features of the West European and Atlantic regional systems, analyzes the influences of the major determinative factors involved, and projects the more and the less probable ways in which they will affect the evolution of the European Community and of the Atlantic region as a whole in the years to come. It deals not only with the relevant economic and political interests, arrangements and problems but also with the perceptions of them by North Americans and West Europeans and their conceptions of how the European and Atlantic systems should evolve in the future.

Most of this report is condensed from Chapters V and VI of the author's forthcoming book, *The Fortunes of the West: Continuity and Change in the Future of the Atlantic Nations*. All of the subjects treated here, as well as many others related to them, are more fully analyzed in the larger study.

Before turning to these subjects, however, three terms need to be defined. They are *integration*, *unification* and *union*. Although their use as broadly synonymous would be grammatically justified, this practice has resulted in considerable confusion and the dissemination of unduly optimistic or pessimistic expectations by political leaders, journalists and even some scholars. Distinctions among these terms are desirable because they point to real differences in the nature and degree of probability of the possible economic and political relationships among Atlantic countries.

The term *integration* is used here in an economic sense to denote the removal of barriers to trade and payments among a group of countries so that, at the end of the process, goods and money move freely across national political boundaries. Integration does not involve transfers of sovereignty to supranational agencies even though the national governments concerned do lose a substantial degree of freedom of action in consequence of their mutual contractual obligations to eliminate and not thereafter restore such barriers, and of their voluntary efforts to co-ordinate their national economic policies. The term *unification* is used to denote a process — economic, political or military — that does require deliberate delegation of important sovereign powers to supranational authorities in one or more of these fields. The related term *union* is used as the ultimate goal of a unification movement — that is, a full federal union of formerly independent countries. Thus, in modern, industrialized nation-states, political and economic unification must of necessity involve economic integration, but the converse is not true even though the latter process may eventuate in the former. The characteristic that distinguishes the two processes is the degree of supranationality, that is, the extent to which the sovereignty of the individual nation-states participating in them is delegated to, or otherwise acquired by, superordinate authorities.

THEODORE GEIGER
National Planning Association
Washington, D.C.
October, 1970

I The postwar restructuring of Western Europe and the Atlantic region

During the postwar period —roughly the two decades from the end of World War II until the mid-1960s —major changes were made in the political and economic relationships among the nations of Western Europe and between them and North America. This restructuring of Atlantic relations was one result of the fact that, in those years, there were both a need to reconstitute the entire international system and a worldwide expectation that it would be different from and better than that of the prewar period. The two existing superpowers —the United States and the Soviet Union— possessed in varying, though sufficient, degree the military strength and the economic resources required to provide leadership in this task. Each of the superpowers had a radically different and competing design of the kind of world order it wished to institute and was strongly motivated both by national interest and by sense of mission to take the initiative in organizing the new system. Moreover, their mutual distrust strengthened the conviction of each that not only its welfare but its very survival depended on thwarting the other's design and advancing its own.

As it took shape during and after World War II, U.S. policy envisaged a worldwide system of large, medium and small states, brought into existence by the principle of self-determination, respecting each others' sovereign independence, governed by increasingly democratic regimes dedicated to improving the economic and social welfare of their people, and conducting mutually beneficial economic and cultural relations with one another. This conception of a permanently peaceful and progressing world order reflected the rationalistic and legalistic biases of American culture and the unique historical experiences of the United States. These elements also fostered the American conviction that the benefits of the U.S. design for a transformed international system were self-evident and, therefore, every enlightened and responsible nation could not fail in its own interest to help achieve it. With their faith in the power of reason validated by their own unprecedented technological accomplishments, Americans were inclined to believe that, with the spread of science and education, the ranks of such rational nations would irresistibly grow. Thus, the inevitability of progress would guarantee the evolution of a rational world order.

Although most Europeans did not share a comparable faith in the efficacy of reason and science, they too were convinced that the deep troubles of the prewar years —aggression, oppression, depression— had to be avoided by major changes in the relationships among nations. Moreover, they felt a similar fear of the catastrophic danger perceived in the Soviet Union's competing design for a new world order. In consequence, the West European countries were willing to join with the United States in the task of restructuring both the European and the Atlantic regional systems. The results of this joint transatlantic effort were the achievement of unprecedented degrees of economic integration within Western Europe and in the Atlantic region as a whole, and the parallel and related political and military arrangements for mutual defense against the external menace of the Soviet Union.

These institutional changes were shaped not only by immediately perceived needs and interests but also by certain longer-term conceptions of the desirable organization of Western Europe and of the Atlantic region. And, both the existing structural relationships within Western Europe and the Atlantic region and these expectations regarding their future evolution are playing major roles in determining the course of development during the 1970s. Hence, in order to assess the problems and prospects of transatlantic relationships in the years to come, we need to analyze briefly the main aspects of the continuing trends in Western Europe and the Atlantic region as they have developed during and since the postwar period.

The Roots of the European Unification Movement

In the light of Western Europe's current prosperity and continued rapid economic growth, it is difficult to recapture today the deep pessimism regarding continental Europe's future that permeated both European and American perceptions and ways of thinking in the late 1940s. On both sides of the Atlantic, there was a growing conviction that the source of Western Europe's problems was the inadequacy of its basic constitution —its division into small nation-states. Several elements contributed to this conclusion.

The first was a strong retrospective sense in the continental countries of the failure of the European nation-state system during the first half of the 20th century. The senseless slaughter of World War I and the subsequent ineffectualness of the political and economic arrangements established by the Versailles settlement; the interwar rise and triumph of Italian fascism and German Nazism; the great depression of the 1930s and the inability of national economic policies to prevent or overcome it; the ease of Nazi conquest at the outbreak of World War II, the shame of German occupation, and the humiliation implicit in having to be liberated by the Anglo-Americans and the Russians; finally, in Germany, the guilt for Nazi atrocities and the trauma of total defeat — these and related experiences of the period 1914-45 undermined traditional continental confidence in the superiority of European culture and the effectiveness of European institutions.

Superimposed upon this sense of past failures was the manifest inability of the nation-state to cope with the problems of the immediate postwar years. It would be difficult to say in which dimension —economic, political or military— continental Europeans felt that the inadequacies of the existing national systems were greater or more dangerous for their security and welfare.

Owing to the destruction and disruption of the war, the continental countries were unable to meet their minimum consumption and reconstruction needs directly from their own production or indirectly by exporting goods and services to pay for necessary imports. In consequence, the rationing of food, fuel, raw materials and other products had to be continued after the war, and in some countries was more restrictive than during the wartime years. A series of emergency relief programs financed by the United States was started even before the end of the war to provide the required imports of consumers' goods and of fuel, raw materials and replacement parts so that undamaged and readily repairable European factories could maintain or resume production. These emergency relief efforts were replaced in 1948 by the European Recovery Program (ERP) — the Marshall Plan — which aimed within a four-year period to rebuild European productive capacity to the prewar level and, through capital investment and technical improvement, to lay the foundations for continuing increases in productivity and output.

Although the ERP achieved its goal, reaching prewar production levels even before its scheduled end, the predominant view both in Western Europe and in the United States was that the West European economies would continue to require American assistance for the indefinite future owing to their inherent weaknesses. It was widely believed on both sides of the Atlantic that lagging productivity, inadequate competitive ability, restricted economic opportunities in small rigidified national markets, nondynamic entrepreneurial attitudes, liquidation of overseas investments, worsening terms of trade, and other economic changes adverse to Western Europe would persist for the indefinite future, resulting in technological stagnation, inflation, balance-of-payments deficits, and continued need for American aid.

The difficulty of coping with existing economic problems and the pessimism regarding the economic outlook for the future were intensified by internal political instability and uncertainty. In two of the major continental countries, France and Italy, as well as in some of the smaller nations, extremist groups of the left and the right were active and growing during the immediate postwar years. Barely able to suppress street rioting and other outbreaks of violence by these extremist groups, the governing coalitions of center parties in several of these countries were unstable and short-lived. They were unable to agree upon policies capable of meeting pressing economic needs and to implement vigorously those measures upon which they could agree. Seriously threatened from within and seemingly able to do little more than maintain routine administration, the centrist coalitions gave the appearance of being caretaker governments that were sooner or later bound to be swept away by extremist movements or to collapse of their own factionalism and ineffectualness. Indeed, it is far from clear how much of the communist failure to seize power in some countries during those years was owed to the strength of the political and economic institutions surviving from the interwar period, as compared to the poor leadership and subservience to Soviet control of the West European

Communist Parties and the unwillingness of the Soviet Union to back them at the cost of war with the United States.

Reflecting and compounding the severity of these economic and political weaknesses was the alarming inability of the continental West European countries to make a significant contribution to their own defense during the dangerous years of the developing cold war. None possessed the resources or the technology needed to make nuclear weapons, and even the raising and equipping of conventional forces were beyond their capabilities. The insurrection of the communists in Greece and their seizure of power in Czechoslovakia, the Berlin blockade and other initiatives and responses by the Soviet Union, and —most important of all— the outbreak of the Korean War engendered a pervasive sense that Western Europe was in imminent danger of becoming the nuclear battleground of the third world war, which it was powerless to prevent and in which it would be incapable of defending itself.

As characterized in an analysis written at the time by the author and a colleague in the Marshall Plan, the effects on West European morale of these postwar difficulties and crises, superimposed upon the retrospective sense of European failure, amounted to:

> 'a conviction —not always clearly articulated but felt nonetheless strongly— that the national political and economic structure of the continent is simply not adequate to cope with the rigorous world environment of the mid-twentieth century. . . . The average continental European feels himself a member of an enfeebled nation, the nearly helpless prize in a world power struggle in which his government plays no effective part. He knows that his economic horizons, his freedom of movement and opportunity are constricted within narrow national boundaries. He believes that the major factors determining his economic well-being, his military security and even his personal survival are beyond the capacity of his government to control or even to influence very much. Unlike the average American or Briton, he feels that his national state is no longer capable of adequately discharging the increasingly heavy responsibilities of political sovereignty. As a consequence, and no matter how much the traditions and culture of his society still mean to him, his belief in and loyalty to his government as a sovereign political entity, his willingness to sacrifice and, if necessary, to die for it have been very severely impaired.' *

The widespread sense in continental Western Europe of the past failure and current incapacity of the nation-state was reinforced by the conviction that European nationalism, the major cause of serious wars in past centuries, had to be superseded or securely constrained if world peace was to prevail. In the perspective of recent wars, this meant essentially an enduring reconciliation of France and Germany. Moreover, in the immediate postwar years, there was already a growing concern that Germany had to

*Theodore Geiger and H. van B. Cleveland, *Making Western Europe Defensible* (Washington, D.C.: National Planning Association, 1951) pp. 43-44.

be firmly integrated into Western Europe lest it sooner or later come under Soviet control.

These convictions about the inadequacy of the existing European nation-state system provided the incentive and the opportunity on both sides of the Atlantic for initiatives aimed at reconstituting on a new basis the structural and functional relationships of the Atlantic region. Americans were as concerned about these needs and possibilities as were Europeans, and the political, economic and intellectual support of the United States was essential not only for the realization but also for the formulation of the proposals designed to reorganize the regional system. Even by the late 1940s, when it had become clear that the Soviet Union was the main obstacle and danger to the achievement of America's world-transforming goal, fear that conflicting European nationalisms and revived imperial ambitions would again involve the United States in a world war continued to motivate American policy toward Europe. Of more immediate concern was the U.S. fear of imminent communist takeovers, particularly in France and Italy. And, to these defensive motivations was added the growing conviction among Americans involved in U.S. policies and programs for Europe that the latter's internal problems could no longer be dealt with adequately by its small weak nation-states.

Conceptions of European and Atlantic Restructuring

The ideas and arrangements for solving this basic structural problem that were proposed on both sides of the Atlantic during the late 1940s and early 1950s can be divided into two kinds: those involving the unification of Western Europe, and those concerned with the future relationships between a united Europe and North America, that is, for the organization of the Atlantic region as a whole. Each of these concepts embraced a range that varied with respect to the kind and extent of the economic integration and political and military unification envisaged and the nature of the relationship between the two parts of the region that would result therefrom. Moreover, each set was in varying degree both complementary to and incompatible with the other, depending upon the extent of the European or Atlantic unification believed to be required.

The predominant movement in continental Western Europe was inspired by the range of concepts envisioning as its maximum development a United States of Europe — a full federal union. The idea of a single European political entity had, of course, a long history — indeed, going back through medieval Christendom to the universal Roman empire. In its modern form, proposals for a United States of Europe were made by Aristide Briand and other European politicians and political philosophers in the interwar period. Serious discussions of this prescription were carried on during World War II both in the resistance movements in the occupied countries and among people associated with the continental governments-in-exile in England and the United States. In the wake of the liberation, several private organizations were founded to promote various ways of achieving a united Europe. They soon polarized into the alternatives of the *functional* approach, explained below, and the *constitutional* approach, which envisaged the immediate calling of a convention to form a federal union. In 1948, the alternatives were conceptually and organizationally consolidated in the European Movement, whose branches in the various European countries are still active today. Finally, in 1955, the Action Committee for the United States of Europe was formed as a multinational organization bringing together designated representatives of the major (non-communist) European political parties and trade unions under the chairmanship of Jean Monnet.

The theory of functional integration was first propounded by the political scientist David Mitrany during the 1930s as a means of bringing about a new peaceful system of world order. As adapted and applied to the task of uniting Europe by European and American policy planners in the late 1940s and 1950s, the theory essentially argues that, as the extent of economic integration among a group of countries increases, concomitant need and pressure develop for supranational authority. The maintenance of the economic integration already achieved and the management of further progress toward complete economic unification require increasingly close and continuous coordination of national economic policies, the settlement of disputes among the participants, and the formulation and implementation of joint measures to take care of common problems. As the pressure on them grows to carry out these increasingly important functions, the participating governments would be less and less able to agree upon and to implement effectively the necessary policies and actions through negotiation and cooperation. Hence, they would have no choice but to delegate more and more of these responsibilities to nonpolitical, technically qualified agencies at the supranational level. However reluctantly, national governments would be compelled gradually to grant these agencies expanded authority by the need to preserve the manifest benefits of the economic integration already achieved and by the insistence of business, labor, farm and other private groups, whose interests would require further progress in integration. Thus, the longer the integration process continues, the greater the power that would have to be given to supranational authorities, who would thereby acquire more and more political, as well as economic, functions. At a certain point, their growing exercise of supranational power would be formalized through the adoption of a constitution for a federal union.

In this way, the functional and the constitutional approaches to union were reconciled. Although there have been some strategists who have continued to advocate, or have in recent years reverted to, the original constitutional approach, the predominant view in Western Europe has been that functional integration would eventually and inevitably lead to constitutional union.

The other range of concepts developed in the late 1940s and 1950s deals with the restructuring of relationships among Atlantic countries. At its extreme was the movement for Atlantic union. Although it also had advocates during the interwar years, interest in Atlantic union was stimulated in the postwar period by the desire to find an Atlantic-wide alternative to European union. During the 1950s, its period of greatest significance, the Atlantic union movement was predominantly a North American phenomenon with considerable support in the U.S. Congress and American and Canadian business circles and with some adherents in Europe, especially in the United Kingdom. It, too, was envisaged as developing through either functional or constitutional approaches. The majority of Atlanticists had in mind a gradualist functional approach, foreseeing the most likely course of evolution as occurring in NATO through the progressive unification of the armed forces and command structures of the member countries. Military unification would inevitably require close and continuous coordination of foreign policies, on the one hand, and of defense research and production programs, and hence of national economic policies, on the other. Either or both of these processes would lead to the establishment and strengthening of supranational authority which, in turn, would culminate in a formal political union in accordance with the theory of functional-constitutional inevitability.

These two designs for a reconstituted Atlantic region have been in part complementary and in part competitive. The desire to realize the benefits of their mutual supportiveness and to minimize the adverse effects of their inconsistency led many Americans and Europeans to accept a reconciliation of the two sets of prescriptions. This is the idea of Atlantic partnership —an arrangement under which economic policy, foreign policy and defense policy for the Atlantic countries would be made jointly by the United States and a united Europe, able and willing to provide an equitable share of the resources required to carry on the common Atlantic role in the world. In this conception, European union is regarded as an essential precondition for the larger process of Atlantic unification. However, there have been important bodies of opinion on both sides of the Atlantic that have rejected this reconciliation —in Europe because it implied the eventual merging of a European union in Atlantic arrangements which, it was feared, would be dominated by the Americans; and in the United States because it was believed that the formation of a European union would eliminate the need for and the willingness of Europeans to participate in an Atlantic arrangement.

American policy was of crucial importance not only for Atlantic arrangements, in which the United States would participate, but also for European union, in which it would not. During the formative years of the late 1940s and early 1950s, U.S. influence was at its height and the U.S. will was as nearly unquestioned in Western Europe as it has ever been. The continental countries were so weak and dependent on the protection and assistance of the United States that official American opposition to the unification, and even to the economic integration, of Western Europe would have been sufficient to prevent either development. Conversely, the positive support and encouragement of the United States was a necessary precondition for their accomplishment. For, an additional manifestation of the inadequacy of European nation-states was the fact that none of the continental countries possessed the will and ability to provide the requisite leadership toward European unification. In consequence, during the late 1940s and early 1950s, the policy of the U.S. government was determinative, and the support of public opinion within the United States was critically significant.

Progress of European Unification in the Postwar Period

In the immediate postwar years, a new generation of political leaders and civil servants began to reach top-level policy-making positions in continental West European governments. And, it was among them that the sense of the inadequacy of the nation-state was greatest and the concomitant dedication to the unification of Europe was strongest. Robert Schuman and René Pleven in France, Konrad Adenauer and Walter Hallstein in Germany, Alcide de Gasperi in Italy, Paul-Henri Spaak and Paul van Zeeland in Belgium, and J. W. Beyen in the Netherlands are only a few of the better known political leaders who became committed to European unification. In the late 1940s and 1950s, they worked effectively with one another, with the growing group of Europeanists headed by Jean Monnet, and with Americans in launching their countries on the unification process. In consequence of these efforts, the six continental nations — Belgium, France, Germany, Italy, Luxembourg and the Netherlands — became the founding members of the successive institutional arrangements that were intended to evolve inevitably into the United States of Europe.

In contrast to these continental countries, in which the sense of inadequacy of the nation-state system was most deeply felt in the postwar years, the United Kingdom emerged from World War II with the high morale and confidence in the future to be expected in a victor of that conflict. True, in the late 1940s and early 1950s, Britain faced reconstruction tasks and economic recovery difficulties fully as great as those of the continental countries, but its political system was unimpaired. Also, during this period, it was still able to contribute to the exchange of nuclear technology with the United States, and its own military establishment was still large and effective enough to sustain the conviction that it could continue to play a significant role in its own defense and in that of Commonwealth countries and client states throughout the world. Thus, despite their economic problems, the British had a strong sense of the adequacy of *their* nation-state and felt little, if any, need to join with the continental countries in the movement toward a political and economic union. The great majority of the British people at all social levels were convinced that they still possessed the strength and the obligation to play a major role in the world as the leader of a globe-encircling Commonwealth of nations and, through continuation of the 'special relationship', as the closest and most influential ally of the United States. In the Scandinavian countries, too, the sense of inadequacy of the nation-state was not great enough to impel them to active participation in the European unification movement.

In consequence, the scope of European unification was limited to the six continental countries. Their progress toward that goal during the 1950s culminated in the Treaty of Rome, which went into effect on January 1, 1958. It provided in detail for the gradual formation during a 12-year period, terminating on January 1, 1970, of the European Economic Community (EEC), which would be a customs union among the six member countries. Despite the difficulties encountered during the mid-1960s in the negotiation of a common agricultural policy — the precondition for free trade in agricultural products — and the problems posed by de Gaulle's opposition to supranationality, the Six were able to accelerate to July 1, 1968 the achievement of their customs union. Moreover, in the same year, agreement was reached to merge the central agencies of the EEC and of the already existing European Coal and Steel Community (ECSC) and European Atomic Energy Community (Euratom) into a single European Community (EC). *

The Treaty of Rome also envisaged that the customs union would in turn be only a transitional phase to a full economic union. It would gradually be achieved by adoption of common policies and regulations in all fields significant for intra-Community competition, abolition of the remaining barriers to the free movement not only of goods but also of capital, labor and enterprise, and development of a unified system of money and banking for the region as a whole. To foster this progressive unification movement, as well as to manage the process of forming and preserving the customs union, the Treaty established the European Commission endowed with certain supranational powers. However, the Treaty did not specify in detail — as it had for the customs union — the steps and a timetable for achieving the full economic union or the political preconditions for and consequences of its attainment. The problems involved in the EC's moving beyond the customs union to full economic union and eventually to political federation and the likelihood that these developments will occur are discussed in Chapter II.

Because economic and political unification was from the beginning the aim of the EC's founders, neither the United Kingdom nor the Scandinavian countries were willing to participate in its establishment. Nevertheless, they recognized the advantages of membership in a large free-trade arrangement and feared the possible adverse consequences for their own exports of the trade-diverting effects of the formation of the EC. To obtain the benefits of economic integration without supranationality and unification objectives, the British initially proposed the formation of a European-

*As the official name for the institution is now the European Community, the abbreviation EC will be used in this report rather than the obsolete form EEC or the colloquial term Common Market.

wide free-trade area to include the EC. When this proposal was rejected by the Six as an effort to sabotage the EC, the United Kingdom joined with Austria, Denmark, Norway, Portugal, Sweden and Switzerland (with Finland and Iceland later participating as associate members) to form the European Free Trade Association (EFTA) in 1960. The EFTA obtained a waiver from the General Agreement on Tariffs and Trade (GATT) permitting its members to retain trade restrictions on most agricultural products, thereby avoiding the difficulties faced in this area by the EC and making it possible for the members to achieve internal freedom of trade affecting industrial products by January 1, 1967. The success of the EFTA demonstrated that a free-trade arrangement could be operated without either the common external tariff or the coordinated national economic policies of a customs union and with a simple institutional structure lacking supranational powers and having a minimum of formalized rules and regulations for maintaining free trade and handling the problems and disputes involved.

The EFTA's progress during the 1960s was all the more noteworthy because its existence was in doubt throughout the period of its successful movement to free trade in industrial products. Although initially proposing EFTA as an alternative to a supranational arrangement, the United Kingdom, the leading member, soon reversed its policy toward European unification. In 1961, it started negotiations regarding terms of membership in the EC. The British example was immediately followed by several other EFTA members. This change in British policy in large part reflected the United Kingdom's increasingly serious problems of internal adjustment and external balance that were already becoming evident in the early 1960s. But, in part, the decisions of the United Kingdom and other EFTA countries to seek membership in the EC were also influenced by the sense of progress and the growing prestige that characterized it in those years.

For, the early 1960s were the high-water mark of the European unification movement. The EC's six members were then enjoying unusually rapid rates of economic growth, expanding trade, rising living standards, full —indeed, overfull— employment, increasing monetary reserves, and a pervasive feeling of economic well-being and continuing momentum. Their joint efforts to meet the schedule for establishing the customs union specified in the Treaty of Rome and to work out the policy measures required for it were being conducted in the 'Community spirit', as it was called, of willingness to subordinate national interests to the new interest of the common objective, a united Europe. And, conflicts of national interests that in other circumstances would have been irreconcilable were in fact settled in the spirit of community. In turn, these successes further strengthened the sense of progress and the conviction —not only among the Six but also in the other Atlantic nations— that the EC was advancing rapidly in the unification process, which would irresistibly bring it to full economic and political union in the foreseeable future.

So great was the self-confidence and *élan* of the EC in those years and so high its prestige that the attitudes toward it of the other Atlantic countries were correspondingly affected. Not only did the United Kingdom and other European nations apply for membership in the EC but, equally significant, the United States regarded it with mounting respect, and even with some concern. For those in the U.S. government and in private life who had fought for and carried out the American commitment to support European union, the progress of the EC and the prospect that it would soon be enlarged to include the United Kingdom and other European nations vindicated their faith and their efforts. Among official policy makers in Washington and opinion leaders throughout the country, there was growing agreement that the United States would have to adapt its economic, political and military relationships to the new capabilities and challenging potentials of a united Europe. It was this reaction in the United States that led in 1962 to official proclamation of the 'Grand Design' for Atlantic partnership, under which the U.S. government offered —verbally, at any rate— to share equally with a united Europe in the responsibilities and costs of managing the security and progress of the 'Free World'. Thus, in the early years of the 1960s, it seemed that both the Europeans' goal of union and the Americans' goal of partnership were at long last within reach.

The Development of Atlantic Economic Integration

Parallel to and in part made possible by the process of European integration has been the increasing economic integration of the Atlantic region as a whole since the late 1950s.

In the degree and significance of its integration, the contemporary Atlantic economic system resembles the worldwide economy that endured from the adoption of free trade by Great Britain in the mid-19th century until World War I. However, there are certain differences between the two integrated systems both in structure and in the means by which each maintains its substantial degree of openness. Economic integration involves the continuous mutual adjustment of conditions and trends in the constituent national economies at both *macro* (the economy as a whole) and *micro* (individual producing, consuming and investing units) levels. During the 19th century, such continuous adjustments took place regardless of their adverse effects on each country's rate of economic growth, level of employment, pattern of production, distribution of income, and standard of living. Today, governments seek individually and in concert to manage the adjustment process so as to prevent it from affecting these aspects of national economic welfare in ways no longer acceptable to their opinion leaders and their people generally.

Thus, the differences in the means by which each system preserves economic integration stem largely from the major changes in attitudes and expectations and in economic knowledge between the second half of the 19th century and the second half of the 20th century. These changes within

Atlantic societies, especially in their contemporary manifestations, are of such immense complexity and depth as to defy generalizing about them with reasonable accuracy. Suffice it to say, they are today reflected in the unprecedented diversity and scale of the goals that the people of Atlantic countries now believe must be realized as quickly as possible and no longer regard merely as ideals to be achieved, if ever, in some far-distant future. This revolution in basic attitudes and values has had the effect of adding new functions and responsibilities to those hitherto believed necessary and proper for governments and private institutions to perform.

In addition to their previous activities, governments now seek to provide minimum incomes and equal opportunities to all, assure rising standards of education and health, protect and improve the physical environment, rebuild the cities, foster and finance the advancement of knowledge, support the arts, expand recreational facilities to meet greater leisure and earlier retirement, and in a growing variety of other ways better the quality of life for an increasing population. These new needs and expectations are being met not only by expanding the public sector, but also by enlisting, pressuring and regulating the private sector. In varying degree, business firms, too, are helping to improve the environment, renovate the slums, support education, science and the arts; the universities are acting to reform, and not simply prescribing for, the ills of society; and the churches are trying to make the secular city like the heavenly one. There is not a major institution in Atlantic societies that, voluntarily or perforce, is not broadening its conception of its appropriate functions.

One of the many ironies of our fascinating age is that those who, in the name of higher values, deplore the importance attached to rapid economic growth are themselves among the main perpetrators of the intensified pressures for increasing resources. The fact of the matter is that there are few, if any, among the proliferating values that Atlantic societies are now trying to realize which do not require greater economic resources in one form or another. And, the effort to achieve such goals is practicable for the first time in human history only because the industralized economies of the Atlantic countries are so productive and have grown so fast. Moreover, the unprecedented productivity of Atlantic economic systems depends upon their size, flexibility and diversification, upon their intricate and highly interdependent division of labor, upon their vast mechanization and spreading automation, and upon the sophisticated knowledge, skills and motivations that animate them. Assuring the growth and the internal and external equilibrium of these immense, complex economic systems are not least among the more difficult functions that Atlantic governments are now increasingly performing.

The interest of the member nations in maintaining and extending the economic integration of the Atlantic region arises essentially from this central importance of economic growth in contemporary Atlantic societies. Traditional economic theory has long recognized the relationship between foreign trade and resource availabilities in its well-known economic principle of the gains from external trade and investment in accordance with the comparative advantages of the national economies involved. Many Atlantic countries are dependent upon foreign commerce both because exports constitute a substantial percentage of their gross national products (GNP) and because of their need to import raw materials lacking in their natural resource endowments and other goods they are unable to make at economical costs. In addition, for certain countries, such as Germany, Italy and Japan, exports have been in some years what economists call the 'engine of growth' —the most buoyant portion of final demand both stimulating and reflecting high levels of production and investment. The benefits to growth of importing and exporting capital have also been substantial for many Atlantic countries.

Moreover, the changes in institutions, values and attitudes during the decades since World War II have given economic growth a greatly enhanced importance. It has become simultaneously the means for obtaining additional resources needed to achieve the proliferating range and increasing size of national goals; a high-priority claimant for resources on its own behalf; and a major contributor to both the causes and the mitigation of the problems of internal and external imbalance that plague Atlantic economies. Hence, the relationship between economic growth and foreign trade and investment has come to be seen in contemporary economic theory as encompassing considerably more than the so-called 'static effects' comprised in the traditional view noted above. These other kinds of gains are usually called the 'dynamic effects'.

Difficult to measure directly, the dynamic effects embrace the various ways in which the freer and bigger flows of goods and capital in an integrated regional system stimulate and sustain the growth rates of its constituent national economies. The enlarged market made available by the openness of comparatively small national economies to one another provides opportunities for new investment and for improving productivity through both the internal economies of scale and the external economies of easier access to cheaper or more diversified ancillary goods and services of all kinds. Equally important are the more intangible and pervasive effects subsumed in the phenomena of regional competition. In addition to the stimulus of competitive imports of goods and services, they include the dynamic effects of competitive development of new products and production and marketing techniques, of competition in devising and applying new organizational arrangements and management methods, and of rivalry to be the first to enter a new market or branch of industry and to be the biggest or the leader in a particular field of production, distribution or finance even though this status may not be the most profitable. In these and other ways, regional competition fosters the self-confidence, initiative, innovation, entrepreneurial vigor, flow of ideas and technologies, and flexibility that are among the major psychosocial components of economic growth in pluralistic societies.

Even for the nearly self-sufficient American economy, whose 50 states constitute the biggest freely trading market on the planet, the opportunities and competitive pressures resulting from its integration into the Atlantic region have been important impulses to its increased dynamism during the 1960s. And, in turn, the various stimuli and competitive influences radiating throughout the region from the United States have been among the most significant factors contributing to the high growth rates of other Atlantic nations —as well as a major source of problems and complaints.

The development of Atlantic economic integration may be briefly sketched.

In consequence of the economic revival stimulated by the Marshall Plan, the general realignment of exchange rates in 1949 and subsequent individual devaluations, the very satisfactory rates of economic growth maintained during the 1950s, and the increasing international availability of dollars resulting from persisting U.S. payments deficits, the West European nations were able to restore the current-account convertibility of their currencies at the end of 1958. Equally significant was the fact that six rounds of tariff-cutting negotiations under GATT auspices, culminating in the Kennedy Round of 1962-67, resulted in a drastic lowering of tariffs affecting trade in industrial products among all of the Atlantic countries, as well as with GATT members in other parts of the world. As a result, when the tariff cuts agreed upon under the Kennedy Round become fully effective by January 1, 1972, the Atlantic region will have a lower level of tariff restrictions on nonagricultural products than before 1914.

Trade liberalization was paralleled by the gradual freeing of short-term capital movements within most of the Atlantic area. In addition, most European countries, and notably the largest capital-exporting nations, the United Kingdom and Germany, liberalized —although they did not completely abolish —their controls on long-term capital movements. However, since the late 1950s, the biggest and most significant component of growing long-term capital flows within the Atlantic region has been the direct investment of American private capital in European industrial, financial and other activities. This has in large part been matched by the movement of long-term European capital to the United States, mainly into portfolio securities but, in recent years, increasingly into direct investment as well. By the beginning of the 1970s, the total accumulated transatlantic long-term private investment was roughly in balance, with American holdings in Europe predominantly direct and European holdings in the United States still mainly portfolio.

The trend toward direct regional investment not only by American companies but increasingly also by European firms reflects several developments and motivations. The first are, of course, the opportunities arising from the high growth rates and increasing purchasing power of Atlantic economies and from the enlarged market areas provided by the two free-trade arrangements in Europe, especially the economically bigger and geographically more concentrated EC. Another is the greater attractiveness for American corporations of manufacturing within the EC and the EFTA compared with trying to export from the United States over their remaining tariff and other barriers against nonmembers. This advantage is reinforced by the savings on transportation and other costs of producing closer to markets, and by the difficulty of most American companies, oriented toward the gigantic U.S home market, of devoting adequate attention and personnel to relatively much smaller export operations. Other important considerations are the desire of American and European companies to keep capital accumulations profitably employed abroad if not at home; and the pressure on American business firms during the 1960s to 'follow the leader' to Europe not only for economic but also for prestige reasons.

In part created by and in turn helping to make possible the high levels of direct regional investment is another major development of the 1960s: the rapid growth of the Eurocurrency market, comprised mostly of dollars with small percentages of readily transferable European currencies. Deposited at interest in European branches of American banks and in local banks, the Eurodollars consist of portions of the official dollar reserves of Atlantic governments, of funds of American and other companies required for or resulting from their expanding direct investments in Europe, of the proceeds of exports by European and Japanese firms to the United States, and of capital from outside the Atlantic region, especially from the oil-rich Middle Eastern countries and Latin America. The total amount of credit, net of redeposits, extended through the Eurodollar market from these sources was estimated at the end of 1969 at $37.5 billion. Thus, by the beginning of the 1970s, this new, flexible, transnational credit facility had grown to become the equivalent of a freely moving international capital market for the Atlantic region similar to that of the 19th century.

Although the competition implicit in economic integration plays an essential role in the growth and welfare of all the Atlantic countries, their attitude toward it is deeply ambivalent. Avid for its benefits, they are unwilling to incur its costs, which are the hardships and the losses involved in the process of continuous mutual adjustment. As noted above, they are no longer willing to meet its costs in the 19th-century way —that is, through periodic depressions, mass unemployment, massive loss of income, widespread bankruptcies of noncompetitive firms and farms, and the unchecked decline of older industries, districts and towns. But, even if it does not entail comparable social disruptions and personal suffering, the price that contemporary Atlantic societies are willing to pay still involves major strains and difficulties. In essence, the momentum of the economic growth process is confronted by the inertia of institutions —their natural resistance to change in their accustomed patterns of internal and external relationships and in their familiar operating procedures. The benefits of economic growth for the majority are weighed against the harm it does to the minority of organizations and individuals unable or unwilling to adapt to changing conditions. Thus, at the *micro* level, the crux of the contemporary ambivalence about regional competition is the understandable reluctance either to make painful adjustments or to accept the undesired consequences of not making them.

The unwillingness of individual producing and consuming units to accept the losses or to forgo the gains of the transfers of income among countries involved in the free flow of goods and capital is reflected and paralleled at the *macro* level by the reluctance of national governments to impair their economic sovereignty — their unilateral ability to influence their national economic conditions and welfare. For, the greater the degree of economic integration, the smaller the freedom of action that participating governments have to respond to the pressures of their people to maximize income gains or to prevent income losses. And, the ambivalence of national governments over the benefits and costs of regional integration is all the greater in the current period, when they are assuming rapidly increasing responsibilities for achieving ever-widening conceptions of desirable national goals.

At bottom, therefore, the difficulty of maintaining and extending regional economic integration so as to help sustain growth and increase welfare reduces itself to the private and governmental resistances to the international transfers of income entailed by the process of continuous mutual adjustments within and among the countries of the Atlantic region. The demands of American business firms and trade unions for protection against imports from Europe, U.S. dissatisfaction with the discriminatory association agreements and restrictive agricultural import policy of the EC, the worries on both sides of the Atlantic about the U.S. balance-of-payments deficit, the fear in Europe of domination by large American corporations, the protests against the various so-called 'gaps' (technological, managerial, education) and the 'brain drain' — these and many other difficulties and complaints are, in essence, only different specific manifestations of the general adjustment problem inherent in the economic integration of the Atlantic region.

In contrast to the 19th-century system, which fatalistically or moralistically accepted much, if not all, of the effects of the adjustment process, the contemporary system both wants to and believes that it can restrict, offset or prevent them. But, efforts to maximize the benefits or to minimize the costs of economic integration inevitably encounter the limitation imposed by the fact that the system lacks an authority capable of deciding upon and enforcing an equitable distribution of income among the countries concerned and the necessary measures of coordinated policy. This is why, difficult as it is, the adjustment problem among the constituent parts of a national economy is inherently much more tractable than it is among the nations comprising a regional economic system. In this basic sense, the effectiveness of the Atlantic system is limited by the absence of a sovereign power. However, the interests of the Atlantic countries in preserving economic integration and the similarity of their institutions, values and norms of behavior have so far been sufficiently great to make possible a reasonably satisfactory degree of voluntary cooperation and coordination of policy. Whether and in what ways they will continue to do so are questions whose possible answers are assessed in Chapter IV.

II The future development of the European Community

The most important question regarding the future of the EC is whether the unification process will continue to the point where a true political and economic union will come into existence. This question is important to the Europeans because they have worked hard and forgone benefits to accomplish the substantial degree of economic integration so far achieved. These efforts and sacrifices are justified not simply by the larger welfare gains already obtained from European integration but also by the very much greater economic, political and psychological benefits expected in the longer term from full European union. The question is important to the United States and Canada both because of the effects on their trade, investment and monetary relations with Western Europe, and because the basic constitution of that region — its politico-economic structure — will be the major factor in determining the nature of its role in the international system and its relationships with North America. Hence, an attempt needs to be made to assess the various influences that will shape the more and the less probable ways in which the EC could develop in the years to come.

The Sense of Adequacy of the Nation-State Today

In Chapter I, the major factors found to be responsible for the origin and postwar development of the movement toward European union were identified as the fears and expectations contributing to the powerful feeling that Europe's then-existing system of comparatively small, weak nation-states was incapable of assuring essential survival needs and of coping with pressing internal problems and external dangers. And, only a strong enough sense of the inadequacy of the nation-state can generate sufficient elite-group pressure and popular support for unification to overcome the inertia of long-established institutions and the opposition of the various groups with vested interests in their perpetuation. While convictions about the adequacy or inadequacy of the nation-state cannot be measured precisely, they can be assessed qualitatively in several ways. Perhaps the simplest and clearest method is to compare the present situation with that of the early postwar years described in Chapter I.

In contrast to the then-pervasive fear of imminent Soviet invasion, very few West Europeans are preoccupied today with worries about impending external aggression. True, suspicion of Russian intentions and apprehension about Soviet military capabilities are still widespread — indeed, they are felt even by some West European Communist Party members and sympathizers. But, these concerns are far less intense and pressing than those of the late 1940s and early 1950s, when the Soviet threat seemed at its height. And, although within the limits of the possible, the development with the highest probability is not that there would be a reversal of Soviet policy in Europe from the essentially defensive stance of the 1960s to the kind of behavior that West Europeans would feel again actively menaced their security and independence.

For reasons beyond the scope of this paper, a fundamental change took place in the nature of the international system that gradually became evident in the course of the 1960s. The main characteristics of the new period of world politics are by now apparent. They are the likelihood of continued mutual deterrence and global competition between two superpowers, pursuing their world-transforming goals by means tending to avoid direct confrontation and to reduce the risk of a third world war; backed by looser, less reliable alliances; and with their rival efforts to manage the international system limited, diffused and weakened by the external initiatives and internal problems of new and old nations in all regions of the planet. In consequence, the international system in the current period is much more stable than during the cold war of the late 1940s and 1950s in the sense that neither of the old superpowers, nor a possible new superpower such as China, is likely in the foreseeable future to be able to alter fundamentally the basic configuration of power relationships —in other words, to achieve world-transforming objectives. But, the international system is as insecure as during the cold-war period in the sense that it remains subject to recurrent political crises that continuously involve the superpowers in actions to advance or protect their conceptions of their national interests and world-transforming missions and that threaten to develop into the kind of dangerous direct confrontations they are trying to avoid.

The implication of these changes for Western Europe has been that, in contrast to the late 1940s and early 1950s when the Europeans felt alarmingly exposed to imminent Soviet invasion, their sense of security has steadily increased during the 1960s. Even the two apparently most directly threatening Soviet moves in the decade —the Berlin Wall crisis of 1961 and the occupation of Czechoslovakia in 1968— were in time seen in Western Europe to be defensive actions designed in large part to counteract the attraction it exerted on the East European members of the Russian hegemony. Hence, it is unlikely that the Soviet Union would switch to an expansionist strategy in Western Europe in the absence of changes in American policy that would encourage such behavior. Possible developments that could restimulate both a more aggressive Soviet policy in Western Europe and the latter's conviction that it had to 'unite or perish' would be a deliberate American withdrawal from European responsibilities or its expulsion from them, or perhaps the unintended erosion of European faith in the U.S. nuclear guarantee to the point where it ceased to be credible to them as a deterrent to Soviet aggression. However, the probability that changes of these kinds will occur is less than that they will not.

Thus, insofar as fear of the Soviet Union persists, the American nuclear guarantee is likely to continue for some time to be sufficiently credible to provide an offsetting reassurance. Nor has another external menace appeared to take the place of the Soviet Union. Efforts to cast the United States in this role have very little credence, and the possibility that China may do so in the future, although acknowledged, has little, if any, present effectiveness. The absence today of an external threat that appears so ominous as to confront Europeans with the need to 'unite or perish' has probably contributed more to restoring faith in the adequacy of the nation-state than any other single factor.

This judgment is not meant to belittle the importance of the positive elements involved in the latter result. Certainly, the changes in political conditions in Western Europe since the early postwar years have enhanced the acceptability of the nation-state. This is true even though domestic political problems persist in some countries, notably France and Italy, and may soon arise in others, such as Spain and Portugal. In general, these difficulties are manifestations of the slowness of political and administrative institutions to adapt to basic changes in attitudes and social relationships, of disagreements over resource allocations, and of the persistence of the older types of class antagonisms. However, no significant body of opinion in the countries concerned believes that these kinds of political problems could be eliminated, or even substantially mitigated, by the transfer of sovereignty from national to supranational institutions. Conversely, internal political revolutions or the seizure of power by communist or fascist parties would be likely to destroy existing regimes, not the nation-state *per se*, and the kind of European unification they might lead to would be that of a Napoleon, a Hitler or a Stalin, not that of a Monnet or a Spaak. Despite strikes and demonstrations, governments in France and Italy have ceased to be regarded as impotent 'caretakers' and are able to assert their authority much more effectively than in the late 1940s and early 1950s. Thus, national governments have much greater political stability and effectiveness today compared with the immediate postwar years.

The major positive reason, however, for the renewed sense of adequacy of European nation-states is their extraordinary success in adopting and carrying out the policies and programs that have contributed so importantly to the region's unprecedented economic growth and rising prosperity. Despite the serious and persistent problems of internal and external imbalance, the economic conditions and prospects of the West European countries are today the opposite of what they appeared to be in the immediate postwar years. This economic reversal is much more complete and dramatic than the political change. There is no question today of the economic viability of West European nations, and the circumstances in which they might again become dependent on American aid are hard to imagine. The economic uncertainty regarding European nation-states no longer relates to sheer economic survival, as in the 1940s, but to whether or not they can preserve and increase the prosperity already achieved without further progress toward European union, or continued Atlantic integration, or both.

These differences between the sense of adequacy of the nation-state at the beginning of the 1970s compared with that of the immediate postwar period also reflect the fact that, during the intervening years, its institutional basis has been very substantially strengthened. In essence, the scope and depth of the involvement of national governments in the economic and social welfare processes of their societies have been steadily increasing in consequence of the basic changes in attitudes and expectations in the Atlantic nations sketched in Chapter I. The persistence of this trend continuously expands the size and activities of national government agencies and intensifies their functional interdependencies with the other major institutional systems of their national societies. This development is of such critical importance for the future evolution of the EC —as it is for all Atlantic countries— that its causes need to be analyzed at greater length.

For the first time in their history, the West Europeans have been enjoying the luxury of being able to worry about the problems of prosperity, about the most effective ways to manage the new wealth they have been creating. Throughout the 1960s their energies have been increasingly focused upon their own domestic concerns —upon maintaining their high rates of economic growth despite labor shortages; upon meeting popular expectations for expanding public investment in roads, schools, hospitals, urban redevelopment, recreational amenities, etc. despite the simultaneous pressures for growing private consumption and the need for a high level of business investment; and upon preserving reasonable price stability and balance-of-payments equilibrium despite full employment of labor and facilities. These difficulties are serious and, as events in France, Italy, the United Kingdom and other West European countries have shown, there are no easy or painless solutions for them. But, in the main, they are the 'pleasant' problems of resource allocation in affluent societies, and not the dismal problems of scarcity and depression. Hence, except in Gaullist France, there has been little disposition, conscious or unconscious, to divert popular attention from them by external initiatives or by alarms about foreign dangers, real or imagined. Indeed, so absorbed have the Europeans been during the 1960s in these national problems, and so little have they felt threatened by situations in other parts of the world, that their attitude may now be characterized as a *new nationalism*.

The great majority of the population in West European countries, includint the United Kingdom, is intent upon the achievement of those national goals primarily affecting their economic and cultural welfare. When they become aware of the competition among national goals, they tend to resent the allocation of resources to those that demonstrably interfere with the maintenance and improvement of their living standards. This is especially marked with respect to objectives and responsibilities beyond their borders that appear to make only small or deferred contributions to domestic welfare. This order of priorities, which strongly favors internal over external and economic and cultural over military and political objectives, is a major source of the popular manifestation of the new nationalism and helps to account for its inward-oriented, passive and defensive character.

Another major source of the new nationalism is the fact that realization of the domestic goals accorded the highest priorities in the popular view is dependent upon the political and administrative institutions of the nation-state in two respects. First, the priorities among goals and the allocation of resources to them are substantially effected through the domestic political process, in which the people participate as individual voters and rank-and-file members of political parties, and through administrative decisions, which can be influenced by popular pressures exerted through trade unions and other kinds of voluntary organizations. Second, since the completion of postwar recovery in the late 1950s made more and more of the required resources available within these countries, the ministries of their national governments have become the principal agents for carrying out the allocations determined in large part by these domestic processes and thereby for assuring that economic and cultural goals would progressively be met. Thus, in the course of the 1960s, the majority of the people have increasingly looked inward to their national political and administrative institutions — rather than outward either to American aid, as in the early postwar years, or to new supranational authorities, as in the late 1950s — for preservation and continued improvement of their economic and cultural welfare.

In essence, therefore, two partly offsetting developments have been underway since the early 1950s. On the one hand, some West European national governments have explicitly relinquished portions of their sovereign power to the supranational authorities of the EC, and most have been voluntarily restricting their freedom of action through the removal of trade and payments barriers and the coordination of national economic policies in the integrated European and Atlantic arrangements. On the other hand, the functions of all national governments have been proliferating, the demand for the benefits they provide has become increasingly insistent, and the sense of popular and elite-group dependence on the agencies administering them much greater. Thus, to use a spatial metaphor, while the nation-state has been shifting some of its sovereign power upward to new supranational and multinational arrangements, its functional effectiveness has been more than proportionally augmented through its greater horizontal spread over and deeper penetration into the vital internal processes of its national society.

Although the popular sense of national identity has been strengthened in these ways, the experiences of the postwar period have nevertheless made many more people conscious of a parallel European identity. The passing of European empires and the rise and conspicuousness of many new nations with non-Western cultures; the disproportionate power and worldwide interests of the two superpowers; and, above all, the progress of the European unification movement have fostered the sense of European identity *vis-à-vis* the rest of the world, including the non-European members of the Atlantic region. However, the commitment to a united Europe of people generally, like their new nationalism, tends to be passive rather than active, protecting rather than aggrandizing. Hence, they are devoted to a united Europe and to their nation-state in a manner that does not regard these two loyalties as incompatible or even as noticeably competitive. And, because both commitments are passive, most people are not prepared to make major sacrifices in terms of their economic and cultural welfare either for their countries individually to play leading roles in world politics or for their governments to press on with the unification of Europe.

Will Functional Integration Necessarily Lead to Union?

If, then, there is no longer in Western Europe a profound and pervasive feeling of the inadequacy of the nation-state, are other factors likely to operate that can restart and sustain the unification process?

As explained in Chapter I, the proponents of European union base their expectations of achieving economic and political union on the theory of functionalism —that is, on the inevitability of increasing unification in consequence of the progressively more self-reinforcing character of this process. Nor can there be any doubt that, up to a point, functionalist theory is both logically valid and empirically verifiable. The experience of economic integration during the postwar decades not only in Western Europe but also in the Atlantic region as a whole certainly demonstrates that this process initiates new and strengthens old pressures at both private and governmental levels for further progress in removing discriminatory policies and practices of all kinds and for greater harmonization of economic conditions among the participating countries. All other things being equal, the self-reinforcing character of functional integration would sooner or later bring about tensions among interests, pressures and problems that could create the willingness and ability to transfer crucial political and economic powers to central authorities. However, necessary as the *ceteris paribus* qualification is for theoretical analysis, it is rarely valid in real-life situations. Many other factors —economic, political, other social-institutional, psychological— besides those involved in the self-reinforcing characteristic of functional integration also exert powerful influences, which cannot be discounted in assessing the future of the EC.

Moreover, functionalist strategy implicitly assumes that national governments and private interests have no choice other than to resolve contradictions and eliminate problems even if these results can be accomplished only by transferring responsibility for them to supranational agencies. That there is a decided preference, and hence a marked tendency, to remove conflicts and difficulties rather than to endure them is undeniable —else the human race would still be living in the trees. But there is no compelling necessity to do so. It is never inevitable that logic and the problem-solving impulse will prevail, only more or less probable. Human history equally demonstrates that people can and do live indefinitely with contradictions and problems. They may lack the knowledge or the resources for solving them. The opposing feelings and interests involved may be in balance. The benefits that would be obtained or the difficulties that would be eliminated may not be sufficiently greater than the sacrifices required to motivate the necessary actions. Thus, the nation-states comprised in the EC, and the other countries that may sooner or later become members of it, may prefer to endure indefinitely some or all of the problems generated by the disparities in economic conditions and the divergences in economic trends among them rather than surrender additional important aspects of their sovereign power to supranational authorities.

Functionalist inevitability is sometimes asserted in the form of the 'either/or' fallacy: either the EC's customs union will move ahead to full economic union or it will surely disintegrate into its original national components. Again, such an outcome is within the limits of the possible but it is not necessarily inherent in the nature of integrated arrangements, such as the EC's customs union or the EFTA's free-trade area. The experience of the latter is especially illuminating in this respect. The EFTA's members have been willing to live with the ill effects of many disparate conditions and divergent trends while maintaining their free-trade area. Problems that are felt to be so serious as to require joint action have been dealt with on an *ad hoc* basis rather than by the adoption of a comprehensive set of common policies or the establishment of a supranational authority. If the EFTA is dissolved in the next few years, such an outcome is likely to result not from its failure to move ahead in the integration process but from the decisions of some or all of its members that the advantages of belonging to a very much larger free-trade arrangement like the EC are greater than those obtainable in the EFTA.

The situation is more complex with respect to the possible development of the EC. Both by its founders and by its charter, the EC is intended to engage in a continuing process of economic unification. The Treaty of Rome envisages that the EC will take further steps in economic unification by harmonizing taxation and social welfare charges; adopting common policies regulating transportation and energy and common standards of product quality and safety in important industries; equalizing in other ways the cost factors affecting intercountry competition; and facilitating the establishment of EC-wide companies either through appropriate changes in national laws or by the adoption of a common corporate statute. It is also expected sooner or later to reach agreement on a common currency and to unify capital markets and banking systems. However, there are other courses of development within the limits of the possible. The EC could increase its degree of economic integration in certain respects while refraining from adopting other kinds of measures that would decisively augment the supranational authority of the central institutions — more colloquially, that would push the movement 'over the hump' toward full economic and political union. It could become part of — or could even be superseded by — Atlantic-wide arrangements involving greater economic integration than now exists in the Atlantic region. Or, least likely, it could fail to maintain the existing economic integration of the customs union, reached on July 1, 1968 when internal tariffs were completely abolished and the common external tariff went fully into effect, and dissolve into its constituent national economies.

Supranational Authority Versus Intergovernmental Coordination

So far, the main impairment of national sovereignty in the EC has been renunciation of the right unilaterally to affect national economic conditions by means of tariffs and related barriers to trade. Monetary and fiscal measures, exchange-rate changes, and other policy instruments are still available to member governments at their sole initiative for controlling conditions and trends in their economic systems. Only if and as the unilateral right to use these policy instruments is forgone by member governments will the power of the nation-state be substantially eroded in a functional sense. For, the effects of the institutional strengthening of the nation-state in the past two decades through expanding public investment, social welfare expenditures, and more pervasive regulation of the private sector can be nullified only through major limitation, if not complete surrender, of the power of national governments to control money and credit, the main sources of revenue, and the ways in which it is spent.

In other words, the crucial fiscal decision is not whether larger revenues are allocated to the EC's central institutions but whether they will be given the power *at their own discretion* to levy specified, significantly large taxes and to determine how the proceeds will be spent. Similarly, the crucial monetary decision is not whether the EC's members will maintain permanently fixed exchange rates among themselves as the prelude to a common currency but whether they will be willing to grant a new European central bank (or its equivalent) the power to control the money supply, regulate interest rates and credit availabilities, and manage external monetary relations as necessary preconditions for maintenance of a common currency, that is, for a monetary union. Moreover, delegation of these essential fiscal and monetary powers to supranational authorities would alone focus on them the interested attention and sense of dependence that individuals and organizations of all kinds have been increasingly directing toward their national government agencies in consequence of the growing scope and depth of the latter's functions in the past 20 years.

Nor is it only a question of whether the functions and freedom of action forgone by national governments are central or peripheral to the continued sovereignty of the nation-state. Also significant is whether they are, in fact, granted to supranational authorities or continue to be exercised by national governments themselves but in a manner that more or less coordinates them among the countries concerned. Functionalist strategy envisages that the member governments of the EC will perforce have to delegate broader and broader authority to the Commission. They will have to do so, it is believed, because many of the issues involved in agreeing upon measures of further unification will be so serious as to preclude the possibility of reaching effective compromises, and because the subsequent complexities of implementing them will be too great to be handled by continued intergovernmental cooperation and policy coordination. However, as the experience of the EFTA and the EC shows — and that of the Atlantic region as a whole confirms — cooperation and policy coordination among national governments have not been either too difficult or too inefficient to deal with many critical issues and problems when sufficient willingness to reach agreement exists. And, when it does not, national governments are even less likely to grant a supranational institution the power to impose solutions on them. Rather, they would be prepared to live indefinitely with the difficulties and deficiencies involved.

True, the adoption and carrying out of additional integrating measures in the EC could entail increased administrative responsibilities for the Commission and the secretariat, and probably also greater scope for discretionary judgment and even the disbursement of larger funds. But, these increased functions need not necessarily augment the supranational authority of the EC's central institutions. The national governments could still retain preponderant power. In recent years, new proposals and difficult issues within the EC have tended to be initiated and settled in the Council of Ministers by agreement among the national representatives. Their implementation has often been arranged through coordinated actions of national governments and not by delegating new increments of supranational authority to the Commission. Hence, if the EC's process of economic integration continues in some at least of the fields indicated above, its member governments could decide to do so by using the Commission and secretariat as technical agents administering agreements under the watchful supervision of the national representatives. Moreover, even the move to decision making in the Council by majority vote instead of unanimity does not fundamentally impair national sovereignty, although it may be felt to restrict it unduly by any member in the minority on a particular issue. Once again, it is important to emphasize the difference between the limitation of national sovereignty through intergovernmental cooperation and coordination of policies and activities, on the one hand, and the delegation of portions of the sovereign power to make and implement policies to a supranational authority, on the other.

That conditions and trends are more likely to be conducive to the former than to the latter method of intensifying economic integration in the EC is foreshadowed by the growing resistance of government ministries and national civil servants to further substantial transfers of their functions to the Commission in Brussels. Reflecting not only a natural bureaucratic reluctance to lose authority but also the further institutional strengthening of the nation-state since the late 1950s, this tendency has been especially pronounced with respect to the new governmental responsibilities for the problems of resource allocation and price stability, for the major fields of public investment, and for the expanding social welfare programs. Moreover, the national officials and civil servants who carry on these increasingly important and specialized activities tend to be younger, more professionally trained and activistic technocrats. Although most of them favor European union as a rational goal, national bureaucrats are nevertheless rivals of the Eurocrats in Brussels, and they are not likely to surrender their power and functions to the latter in the absence of strong pressures on them to do so from ministers and politicians, from special-interest groups, or from public opinion generally. Their unwillingness to 'put themselves out of business' is one major reason for the apparent interminability of the negotiations they have been conducting since the early 1960s to formulate common EC policies in several of the various fields envisioned by the Treaty of Rome —e.g., energy, transportation, taxation and social security charges, patents, company law, food and drug regulation, etc.

The other major reason for the slowness of member governments to agree upon and implement these and other common policies is the fact that the pressures for their adoption that functionalist theory assumed would inexorably work for increasing economic unification are not oriented solely and cumulatively toward that end. In practice, both the national and the private interests involved are ambivalent —that is, the rational considerations at stake are not decisively on the side of unification. On the one hand, the benefits of further economic integration and the obligations they have undertaken to advance it impel national governments to consider seriously the proposals for common policies prepared by the Commission and secretariat in Brussels and to participate conscientiously in the negotiations concerning them. Private business firms, too, recognize the advantages for them of the equalization of the conditions of competition within the EC that is the general aim of many of these common policies. On the other hand, further economic unification would mean equivalent losses or limitations of authority by national governments over important aspects of their economic systems and social welfare processes, which they would be unwilling to accept for fear that they would then be unable to fulfill their basic responsibility for assuring national survival and well-being. Similarly, private interests are reluctant to forgo the benefits they have been deriving from differences in national conditions and policies, which generally have the effect of discriminating in their favor. The familiar bird in the hand is often believed to be worth more than the as yet unknown birds in the bush.

The various difficulties and limitations, sketched so far in this chapter, that have slowed the unification process since the mid-1960s have led, especially in Brussels, to a more realistic conception of the self-reinforcing power of functional integration. In effect, the Commission and secretariat no longer pin their hopes of achieving union on the irresistibility of functional integration. Indeed, they now count on its opposite: in place of the logical determinism of functional inevitability, they look to unanticipated disruptions to provide opportunities for effectuating further integration in unpredictable ways. Thus, having tacitly opposed British membership in the EC during the 1960s because it might have changed or delayed the plan and timetable of unification provided in the Treaty of Rome, the Eurocrats in Brussels now favor it precisely because the negotiations might sufficiently disrupt the existing pattern of nearly static relationships to enable new advances to be made.

The Political Perplexities of European Union

The ambivalences of national and private interests explained above are substantially magnified by the political and psychocultural elements also inherent in the process of further unification. For, the greater the authority that is acquired by the supranational institutions in Brussels, the more critical the question of who will control them becomes. It is a tribute to the good sense of contemporary West Europeans, as well as a sign of the passing of the older form of xenophobic nationalism, that so little has been written or spoken on this crucial aspect of European unification. Nevertheless, the uncertainties involved are major considerations in the minds of many political and opinion leaders in Western Europe, as well as of the people generally.

So far, the issue has not arisen in a positive sense, although there were some complaints of excessive French influence in the early 1960s. Nevertheless, the question of ultimate political control has been important negatively in inhibiting agreement on measures of further unification that might otherwise have been adopted. Thus, it has been, and is likely to continue to be, one of the three main obstacles to the formation of a European nuclear force—the others being the unwillingness to divert substantial resources from nonmilitary national goals to this purpose and the persisting, albeit diminished, credibility of the U.S. nuclear guarantee. The political uncertainty also contributes strongly to the reluctance to discuss seriously, much less to agree upon, the transfer of the crucial fiscal and monetary powers to the Commission or to new supranational agencies. For, once the central institutions acquire the military power of control over nuclear weapons and the economic power to tax and regulate money and credit, they would possess the external and internal essentials of political sovereignty. The constituent national society or elite group able to exercise the preponderant influence owing to its size, wealth, dynamism or skill would sooner or later dominate the emerging union.

The issue of political control is usually discussed by the proponents of European union as though it were simply a matter of establishing at the proper time the necessary constitutional arrangements for some form of popular election of a European parliament and for supervision by it of the Commission or a successor European executive. They envisage that the political aspect of this change would involve the transfer of domestic politics to the supranational level —that is, the various national political parties would coalesce in accordance with their conservative, centrist or radical orientations, and European politics would thereafter consist of the same kinds of interest-group competition and bargaining, and disagreements over goals and resource allocations that now constitute much of the substance of national politics. And, it is probable that such a trend would develop, as presaged by the fact that, in the existing advisory European Parliament, the representatives sit in accordance with partisan, not national, affiliations.

However, this aspect of the process of political unification is already, and will continue to be, permeated, distorted and partly offset by another trend that reflects the momentum of national institutions, interests and senses of identity in the period of the new nationalism. This second trend began to manifest itself in the mid-1960s — initially in the bitterness engendered by de Gaulle's veto of British membership in 1963; more strongly in the contentious and prolonged negotiations over the price provisions of the common agricultural policy in 1964; and fully in the so-called 'crisis of 1965' over the financial arrangements for the common agricultural policy and the underlying issues of Commission versus national government responsibilities and functions. One important casualty of these experiences was the 'Community spirit' of subordinating national interests to the common purpose that, as explained in the first chapter, had played so crucial a role in the progress of the EC during its early years. It was customary to attribute not only the specific timing and mode of expression of this nationalizing trend but also its cause to General de Gaulle and to expect that the 'Community spirit' would be revived after his departure from office. The fact that this trend has not vanished or even substantially diminished since de Gaulle's resignation would indicate that it is rooted not in the General's personality but in the attitudinal and institutional changes that characterize the new European nationalism.

Indeed, the trend toward nationalized politics will probably strengthen rather than diminish in the years to come because it is fostered both by the existing institutional arrangements of the EC and by the unlikelihood that a popularly elected European parliament with effective powers would be established soon enough for it to stimulate sufficiently the offsetting first trend toward Europeanized politics. Reflecting and in turn reinforcing the second trend since the mid-1960s, the Council of Ministers, consisting of member government representatives, has increasingly asserted its influence over the supranational Commission which, in consequence, has been playing less of a leadership and policy-making role and becoming more of a technical planning, implementing and advisory agency. This development facilitates the expression of national interests and bargaining power in the Council and the application of national pressures on the Commission and secretariat. In contrast, the existing European Parliament — even though it is composed of national representatives sitting in accordance with partisan affiliations — has no legislative powers and can only review the work of the Commission and make recommendations to the Council. Although it could expose and deplore a growing exercise of national influence, it lacks authority that would permit it to counterbalance, if not to arrest, the trend toward nationalized politics. And, as that trend strengthens, it would make less and less likely the granting of effective powers to the Parliament.

It is probable, too, that the expansion of the EC's membership, through the addition of the United Kingdom, Denmark, Norway, Ireland and perhaps others would also inhibit the development of the first trend toward Europeanized politics. These countries did not experience in the postwar period a sense of the inadequacy of the nation-state comparable to that of the EC's founding members. Nor have the serious economic problems of the United Kingdom during the 1960s generated such feelings among the British people. Despite the professed commitment of the majority of the British elites to European political and economic union, it is more likely that the United Kingdom and the Scandinavian countries would help to slow down the unification process after joining the EC than that they would try to accelerate the transfer by their national governments of sovereign powers to supranational agencies.

In the last analysis, neither the British nor the French nor the Germans would be willing to participate in a European union dominated by one of them. Yet, it is hard to believe that three such identity-conscious, former great powers as France, Germany and the United Kingdom have so lost their sense of vocational mission and conviction of superiority that their younger activistic elite groups would refrain in the years to come from trying to use their size, prestige, economic power and organizational skills to compete for the leadership position in an emerging union. Nor, for all their genuine devotion to the unification goal, is it likely that the smaller European countries would continue to press for its achievement if such rivalry of the big three for preponderant influence were to become evident. While they might reluctantly acquiesce in British domination of the union should a true Europeanized politics fail to become preponderant, they certainly would not find French hegemony acceptable and German even less so. Moreover, the trend has been, and is likely to continue to be, for Germany to become stronger and France and the United Kingdom weaker relative to one another. It is possible that, as many Europeanists envisage, the latter two could cooperate to control the former, but their willingness and ability to do so are by no means assured. Although this possibility reduces the political uncertainty, it does not lower it to the point where the fears of Europeans would be stilled. At bottom, most Europeans are aware that the United States is their ultimate protector not only against the Soviet Union but also against a resurgence of German expansionism. Hence, they are not likely to sacrifice comparatively disinterested American support for the sake of membership in a new European superpower dominated by France or even the United Kingdom, and much less by Germany.

In sum, the uncertainties regarding the issue of political control are major, if relatively unpublicized, factors in European decision making about the future of the unification movement. The lack of assurance regarding the political forces that would dominate an emerging European union is a basic consideration likely to continue to inhibit such steps in political unification as the establishment of a European nuclear force, a popularly elected European parliament with adequate legislative powers, and a more potent unitary, rather than conciliar, European executive. It would surely also deter agreement to confer on the existing interim supranational institutions the additional authority for controlling money and credit, for raising and spending substantial revenues, and for other economic functions that would constitute decisive advances in the movement toward full economic, and hence political, union.

The Role of Relations with the United States in the Unification Process

Another set of influences that have to be taken into account in assessing the prospects for European unification are Western Europe's relationships with the Atlantic region as a whole —which means primarily with the United States. Two aspects most directly related to the foregoing analysis of Europe's ambivalent interests and fears need to be briefly considered.

The first concerns the probabilities for political-military unification. It was stressed above that the improvement of Western Europe's security position, resulting primarily from major changes in the international system as a whole, has substantially lessened the pressure on European countries to develop their own nuclear and conventional military capabilities. This situation results, however, not only from the decline of the Soviet menace but also from the continued existence of the U.S. nuclear guarantee. Indeed, in the latter's absence, the European sense of the adequacy of the nation-state might again decline sufficiently to provide a significant impetus toward unification in the military and political fields. But, there is a dilemma involved that is unlikely to be resolved in a way that fosters European unification. On the one hand, the United States cannot take the risk of explicitly removing its nuclear protection before the Europeans have developed a credible nuclear deterrent of their own. On the other hand, the Europeans need not divert substantial resources to this purpose and risk the political uncertainties of who would control the European nuclear force so long as the United States maintains its nuclear 'umbrella' over them.

In effect, the role of the United States in European unification is today, and for the foreseeable future, the reverse of what it was in the 1940s and '50s. Whereas in the early postwar period the movement toward European union would not have gotten underway without strong American leadership and support, so now even the much reduced U.S. presence in Europe and more qualified commitment to its defense constitute hindrances to the achievement of that goal. For, provided U.S. willingness and ability to defend Western Europe remain credible, they tend to inhibit revival of the sense that the nation-state is inadequate to meet Europe's security needs.

The second aspect of Atlantic relations that enters into the ambivalence of European nations toward further unification is their deep interest in preserving and increasing the substantial degree of economic integration achieved within the Atlantic region as a whole. Whether the EC continues as a more or less integrated customs union or moves ahead toward full economic union, the economic advantages thereby derived would be diminished in relative importance if economic integration among the Atlantic countries as a whole is preserved and especially if it were to become more intensive and effective. The benefits of freer access to an Atlantic-wide market several-fold larger than that of the EC impelled the latter to agree in the Kennedy Round to substantial reductions in its common external tariff. By so doing the EC risked its own integration because the comparative advantages derived by its members from their common external tariff were —and are still —the main immediate economic incentive holding the customs union together. The same ambivalent considerations operate with respect to the reduction and harmonization of nontariff restrictions, a major item on the agendas both for further Atlantic economic integration and for further unification of the EC.

Moreover, the benefits to be derived from the adoption by the EC of some of the common policies and other measures of further unification noted above could equally be obtained by deepening of the already substantial degree of economic integration of the Atlantic region described in Chapters I and IV. The more effectively that the new special drawing rights (SDRs) and the other possible changes in the practices of the International Monetary Fund (IMF) increase international liquidity and facilitate balance-of-payments adjustments among the Atlantic countries, the less pressure there will be on the members of the EC to adopt a common currency and pool their monetary reserves. The more the Eurodollar market grows, the less need there is to unify purely European capital markets. The greater the transnational integration of production in the Atlantic region becomes, the narrower will be the various transatlantic disparities that European union is supposed to eliminate.

Thus, in the years to come, the EC will be under continuing pressure, on the one hand, to preserve and increase Atlantic economic integration by lowering its external barriers to trade and capital flows and coordinating national economic policies, and, on the other hand, to maintain and extend its own internal unification process by harmonizing and equalizing economic conditions within its customs union. Assuring the former means trying to achieve the latter by measures which do not significantly restrict the EC's relations with the other Atlantic countries. And, the more intensive the economic integration at both the Atlantic and the European levels, the more reluctant will the European countries be to give up the benefits of either, and the more difficult will it be to sever the structural links that have developed at each.

The Will to Become a Superpower

The analysis so far in this chapter has examined the main economic and noneconomic factors that seriously counteract the operation of the self-reinforcing characteristic of economic integration. In consequence of them, functionalism constitutes a tendency working toward ultimate union but cannot guarantee that it will inevitably be achieved. For, in the absence of a strong and urgent sense of the inadequacy of the nation-state, the self-reinforcing aspect of economic integration is not powerful enough to overcome the political, psychological and other economic resistances to decisive progress in the unification process.

The question must, therefore, be asked whether there are today, and will for the foreseeable future be, other forces operating in Europe that could sufficiently buttress the self-reinforcing characteristic of economic integration to restart and adequately sustain the movement toward European union. Two more or less related sets of factors may be identified.

The first consists in part of the kinds of problems that certain European politicians and publicists have consciously and unconsciously been dramatizing not only because they have varying degrees of actual importance but also because they express European resentments and insecurities *vis-à-vis* the United States. They are the threats to European independence and prosperity believed to be posed by the various transatlantic 'gaps' — technological, managerial, educational — the 'brain drain', and the spread of large American corporations in Europe; and the related challenge to the supremacy of governments assumed to arise from the growth of 'multinational corporations', not only American but also European. The first set also includes potentially much more serious problems, such as environmental pollution, increasing drug traffic and other transborder forms of crime, burgeoning populations, deteriorating cities, etc. These diverse difficulties are grouped together because the proponents of European union argue that they cannot be dealt with effectively by individual nation-states. Hence, it is claimed, their solution requires adequate supranational authority exercised on a European-wide basis.

Solving, or at least significantly mitigating, problems of these types does in many cases require a broader than national approach. Hence, insofar as they constitute already serious and increasingly important difficulties, as the latter group certainly do, they provide reasons for pressing on with European unification. But, as already explained, union is not the only form of multinational effort. Intergovernmental cooperation and coordination of national policies are also effective, if less efficient, means. In my judgment, none of the above mentioned problems has reached a level of intensity and urgency that would preclude the latter approach. Nor are any or all of them likely to do so in the foreseeable future unless governments perversely refrain from taking both unilateral and joint measures to ameliorate those requiring remedial actions. In other words, the most likely possibility is that there will be a sufficient effort to cope with them by unilateral and cooperative multilateral means to prevent them from reaching a level of intensity and urgency that could only be dealt with by a supranational approach.

The second set of factors would be a much more potent force working toward union. It comprises the basic sociocultural changes that could redirect the sense of mission and the technocratic activism of European elites from domestic concerns to playing a major independent role in world politics, and that could make this reorientation of national purposes acceptable to a majority of the population. The Europeanists argue that European nation-states are too small in terms of population and resources to achieve such a status in world affairs, which could only be attained by a European union. Of all the developments by which a sufficiently strong and pervasive sense of the inadequacy of the nation-state could be revived, this possibility has the highest probability. Yet even for it, the counterbalancing considerations lead to the judgment that the chance of its happening is at best even.

There is no necessary connection between an active independent role in world affairs and European union. In the coming decades, France, Germany and the United Kingdom individually are likely to grow in population to the size, and already possess the technoeconomic capabilities, required for great power status and could, if they were willing, redirect their energies and resources to achieving such an objective. Thus, the essential precondition for an important role in world affairs is willingness to attain it. Even though unification might help to stimulate the will to become a superpower through the greater self-confidence engendered by the strength of numbers and wealth, it is not an essential prerequisite for great power status. Indeed, as the Europeanists' argument itself indicates, the contrary is the case — elite-group and popular willingness to become a superpower is equally a precondition for European union.

Granted this connection, a judgment of relative probabilities depends essentially upon the answers to two questions. First, how much more outward-oriented and activist are European elites likely to become? Second, if they are strongly enough impelled to play a major independent role in world affairs, will they seek to do so on a separate national basis, or through European union, or by arrangements for military and foreign-policy coordination which do not require a decisive transfer of sovereignty to supranational agencies?

As to the first question, it seems probable that the attention and aspirations of European elites would become increasingly outward directed the more successfully they are able to effectuate the internal institutional and other changes needed to make substantial progress toward the domestic goals hitherto accorded the highest priorities. And, it is possible that such developments would satisfy popular expectations sufficiently for the people generally to acquiesce in the reversal of the priorities between achieving domestic welfare objectives and playing important independent roles in world affairs. But, it is at least equally probable that the majority of the population would continue to oppose this shift because the proliferation of wants as resource availabilities increase is an inherent characteristic of affluent Western societies.

Assuming, however, that the people generally would acquiesce in such a reversal of priorities, the second question then becomes relevant. It is by no means certain that a majority of European elites will be convinced that European union is the only effective way to attain an active important world role if they should decide to seek it and are permitted to do so by popular acquiescence. As exemplified by General de Gaulle and his orthodox followers, the European elites most strongly committed to such an objective tend to be the most nationalistic, either opposed to European union or so intent on dominating it as to be likely to arouse the opposition of other members.

For the majority of elites who might be impelled to play an active world role, the fact that the *per capita* cost would be less under a federal union than on a separate national basis would be a rational consideration inducing them to prefer the former. Nonetheless, substantial, if not equal, savings could be obtained under the kind of looser cooperative arrangement for coordinating military forces and foreign policies, noted above, although it would probably be less formidable as a world power. This possibility would be favored by the trends characteristic of the current period of the new nationalism — the passive rather than active commitment to European union by the majority of elites and the people generally, the continued institutional strengthening of the nation-state, the political fears and rivalries impeding unification, and the persisting ambivalence of the various considerations of rational interest involved in full economic integration. Moreover, the longer these trends operate, the more powerfully will they inhibit the kinds of changes in attitudes and institutions needed to generate a strong and widespread enough sense of the imperative necessity of European union for attaining a major role in world politics to give unification a decisive preference over either the independent great power form or the looser coordinated arrangement.

Is the EC Likely to Disintegrate?

Before assessing the net effect of the various factors likely to work for and against European union, a brief comment needs to be made on the contrary possibility that even the existing economic integration would not be maintained and that the EC would dissolve into its constituent national economies. The imaginable circumstances likely to cause such a breach have very low probabilities. One might be that the economic power, military strength and sense of mission of a major member — Germany, for example — would become so disproportionately great and the trend toward nationalized politics so accelerated and preponderant that domination by that nation of the EC would appear imminent. In an effort to avoid being trapped in the kind of relationship that enabled Prussia to control the mid-19th century Zollverein and then to unite Germany politically under its rule, the other members of the EC might try to secede from it. Another unlikely possibility would be a voluntary agreement to dissolve the EC so that the members could obtain the greater benefits of participation in a much larger, emerging Atlantic union. The least likely way in which the EC might be terminated would be as the result of refusal to agree upon, or to meet the demands of a major member—France or the United Kingdom, for example — regarding changes in the common agricultural policy or the adoption of common policies in other important economic fields. That negotiations over such matters will be difficult, prolonged and often bitter is highly probable in view of the experiences of the EC since the mid-1960s. However, it hardly seems within the limits of the possible that member governments would be so quixotic as to sacrifice the substantial advantages their economic systems already derive from the customs union because they are unable to obtain the additional benefits believed to be at stake in negotiations for further integration. Even under de Gaulle, France did not behave in this fashion during the crisis of 1965; at worst, it boycotted many — although not all — meetings of EC bodies until a compromise was reached.

Further Integration Versus Unification

Based on the foregoing analysis, an assessment can now be made of the relative probabilities of the three possible courses of development of the EC. As just explained, by far the least likely is that the EC will disintegrate into its component national economies. Accordingly, the significant evaluation relates to the other two possibilities: (1) that, within the foreseeable future, enough of the crucial fiscal and monetary powers will be transferred to supranational authorities to assure successful completion of the unification process; and (2) that economic integration will continue to broaden and deepen but that it will be sustained by means which do not involve a decisive increase of supranational authority in the EC.

The factors significantly fostering the first possibility are the self-reinforcing characteristic of functional integration; the urge to narrow the disparities between Western Europe and the United States and to increase substantially the former's influence over the economic and political policies and practices of the latter; and the desire of some West European elites for the region to attain superpower status and play an active, independent and important role in world affairs. Offsetting these factors are the decline of the external menace; the strengthening of the institutional base of the nation-state within European countries; the inward focus of popular attention and the strong preference for allocating resources to domestic welfare goals as compared with defense and foreign policy expenditures; the interest in the benefits of continued Atlantic integration and desire to preserve the American nuclear guarantee; and the political uncertainties regarding which member country will in the future exercise the preponderant influence in the EC. The analysis in this chapter leads to the conclusion that, on balance, the trends sustaining the unification process are not likely to be more powerful than those inhibiting it. Hence, the probability that developments decisive for the achievement of European union will occur during the present decade is less than that they will not. In other words, the alternative of continued further economic integration has a greater probability than that of really significant progress toward European union.

Such a course of development enhances the probability that the United Kingdom and other EFTA members, and perhaps eventually Spain and Portugal, would be admitted to membership and, conversely, this geographical expansion would reinforce the factors inhibiting the granting of crucial military and economic powers to supranational authorities.

However, that the ongoing process of EC development will involve further integration and not growing unification is not likely to become clear, or be explicitly accepted, in the shorter term. The ardent advocacy of the Europeanists and the passive commitment of the majority of European elites and of the people to European union mean that this goal will continue to play a major role in European —and American— policy making and opinion formation generally. But, prominent as the terms 'European union', 'federal Europe', 'united Europe', and the rationales purporting to demonstrate the essentiality of unification will consequently be in partisan politics and official pronouncements, their substantive contents and operational implications will relate more and more to actions promoting further integration and less and less to those fostering further unification. Henceforth, measures proposed for adoption by the EC should not be taken at face value, and careful examination is required to determine whether their real significance lies in the former or the latter category.

Proposals for further integration that have a good chance of being accepted sooner or later would include some or all of the following: removal or equalization of the various remaining nontariff barriers; revisions of the common agricultural policy to accelerate the rationalization of European farming and reduce its financial burden; common policies for energy, transportation, communications, health and safety standards, patents, company law, etc.; harmonization of business taxation, social welfare charges, subsidies, procurement practices and other cost factors that significantly affect the conditions of competition within the EC; and, if agreement is reached on reducing or prohibiting exchange-rate fluctuations within the EC, arrangements for providing emergency aid to members in balance-of-payments crises, for unifying national capital markets, and for coordinating more closely the EC's policies on international trade and monetary matters. In many cases, however, such steps would be taken by the adoption of identical or consistent policies and practices by national governments rather than by delegating greater supranational authority to the Commission to devise and enforce the requisite measures of implementation. Instead, the Commission would act as a technical advisor and administering agent for the member governments under the vigilant eyes of the Council of Ministers and its staff.

The further that economic integration proceeds in Western Europe through these and other measures, the greater will be the dynamic tensions that will exist between it and Atlantic economic integration. The Europeans are likely to continue, as they have in the past, to expect concessions from the United States and to press their own interests as strongly as possible. This behavior will express their fears of undue U.S. influence, their anxieties about disproportionate American capabilities, and their increasing desire for more independent and influential roles in regional, if not in global, affairs. However, it will also reflect the disappointment of Europeanists and other members of elite groups over the waning prospects for European union and the related concern that their own sense of European identity might be impaired by increasingly close Atlantic integration. If, as is probable, the EC fails to develop into a true economic and political union by transferring crucial fiscal and monetary powers to supranational authorities, its *raison d'être* in strictly economic terms weakens as Atlantic integration intensifies. Nevertheless, the EC is not likely to be dissolved and efforts to increase its integration abandoned because its economic benefits were declining relative to those simultaneously available in an increasingly integrated Atlantic region, as explained in Chapter IV.

Owing to the interactions between the national and private interests operating in parallel at European and Atlantic levels, the two integration processes are not simply self-reinforcing but also mutually limiting. *Ceteris paribus* — that is, if no other factors, political and sociocultural, were involved — the interrelated processes of economic integration at the two levels would, therefore, reach an equilibrium somewhere in the middle range of the continuum of possible multinational economic arrangements between European union at one extreme and Atlantic union at the other. Thus, the prospects for European integration need in the last analysis to be assessed in the broader context of the future of the Atlantic regional system considered in all of its major dimensions — a task undertaken in the concluding chapter.

III Changing American and Canadian attitudes

Future transatlantic relationships will be shaped not only by the possible developments within Western Europe analyzed in the preceding chapter but also by changes occurring in North America. Accordingly, this chapter sketches in broad outline the trends within the United States and Canada that are likely to continue to affect significantly attitudes regarding their roles in the Atlantic regional system and their expectations with respect to the behavior of the West European nations. Again, these are highly complex subjects, dealing with many interacting movements and counter-movements in the societies and cultures of the two North American countries. Only those aspects of greatest importance for their future participation in the Atlantic regional system can be presented here.

Trends in the United States Affecting Transatlantic Relationships

The dramatic and sometimes alarming developments within the United States in recent years are the distinctive American manifestations of the current transformation of Atlantic societies sketched in Chapter I. Many aspects of this process of profound sociocultural change are being experienced earlier and in more extreme forms in the United States than elsewhere in the Atlantic region.

Certainly, the expansion of the scope and diversity of the values whose realization is now being pressed is most marked in the United States. So, too, are the resulting disputes over national goals and over the priorities among them in the competition for available resources. These controversies are magnified by the mutual fears and resentments among blacks and whites, and by the intensification of the inherently ambivalent feelings between generations that is fostered by rapid social change. And, these conflicts and dissensions tend to be expressed in violent forms in a society whose historical evolution has been so importantly shaped by individual and private-group initiatives, by reformist zeal, and by reliance upon self-help and local cooperation to solve many problems which, in European states, have traditionally been the responsibility of paternalistic, authoritarian central governments.

As elsewhere in the Atlantic region in the period of the new nationalism, one consequence of these developments has been the concentration of American attention and resources on domestic concerns. This shift, however, has not gone as far as in other Atlantic countries owing both to the requirements of the superpower role of the United States and to America's conceptions of its world-transforming mission. But, although these responsibilities and self-conceptions prevent a relapse into isolationism, they too are affected by the changes in American attitudes and expectations, which make U.S. efforts to carry them out more nationalistic than in the postwar period.

The refocusing of American concern and resources on domestic dissensions and needs is only partly responsible for the more nationalistic trend of American foreign policies and actions. Equally important are the effects of external developments on U.S. interests and on America's expectations of achieving substantial progress towards its world-transforming goal. While the impact of changes in the international system on American political and economic interests will be discussed in the next chapter, one conspicuous example may be cited here because it interacts importantly with the effects of such developments on the expectation of progress toward this goal. Owing to the high degree of economic integration already existing in the Atlantic region and the prospective additional reductions in U.S. tariffs as the Kennedy Round cuts are completed, certain business firms and trade unions that are or believe themselves to be adversely affected thereby are pressing for import quota restrictions. Such protectionist reactions from special-interest groups are to be expected and could be dealt with by adjustment assistance and other means not involving the reimposition of tariffs and quotas if it were not for the simultaneous reactions to the frustration of unrealistic American expectations regarding the international system.

The reactions of the opinion-forming elite groups — politicians and government officials, businessmen, trade-union and farm leaders, professionals, scientists, engineers, writers, students, clergymen, teachers, etc. — are deeply ambivalent. On the one hand, the pragmatism characteristic of American culture sooner or later results in adjustments to unwelcome realities and unanticipated setbacks. On the other hand, other characteristics of American culture — the sense of mission, the technocratic faith in the power of reason and science, the parochial assumption that the people of other countries should think and act like Americans — continually generate expectations that even the most intractable problems at home and abroad can be easily and quickly remedied. When the ambivalence is resolved, there is a tendency on the part of opinion leaders, and hence of the public generally, to blame the need to make painful adjustments to reality not on the utopian nature of their goals but on the inadequacy of their own or other people's efforts, and often on the latter's short-sighted selfishness or malign irrationality.*

Such projective reactions of frustration are manifested in the resentment in the United States over the failure of Atlantic relationships to evolve into the kind of partnership envisaged in the Grand Design. Again, the reaction is ambivalent. On the one hand, there is growing recognition that the Grand Design is dead and that efforts to revive it would only be counterproductive. On the other hand, there is widespread exasperation over the

*At bottom, American dissensions over U.S. involvement in the Indochina war are largely conflicts over means, not ends. Those opposing it insist that it is a means inconsistent with America's world-transforming goal; those supporting it claim that it is a means essential for achieving that goal.

presumed refusal of obdurate, self-seeking West European countries to behave in the cooperative ways envisaged by Americans. This is expressed in the feeling that the United States has been 'Uncle Sucker', whose assistance and concessions are unappreciated by Europeans intent upon furthering their own interests at American expense. Reactions of these kinds help to account for the support now being given by many disinterested opinion leaders to the protectionist demands of certain businessmen and trade unionists.

Effects on American Attitudes of the Diminished Prospects for European Union

Another important manifestation of American frustration and resentment over the course of European developments relates to the diminishing prospects for the achievement of European union.

As explained in Chapter I, Americans were willing — indeed, eager — in the postwar period to provide substantial economic aid to Western Europe, and they continue today to make what they believe to be a disproportionate military contribution to European defense, in part because of their conviction that the integration process in Western Europe would culminate in a political and economic union. Moreover, for the sake of European union and its beneficial effects on both sides of the Atlantic, many opinion leaders are convinced that the United States has refrained from advancing its economic and political interests to anywhere near the extent that would have been possible with its preponderant wealth and power. Regardless of whether this view is objectively verifiable, it nevertheless strongly colors American attitudes toward Western Europe. Hence, if American opinion leaders continue to believe that U.S. 'sacrifices' for the cause of European union have been in vain, their disillusionment is bound to exacerbate the already serious disagreements over the specific economic and political issues discussed in the next chapter.

Even granted the significant differences between the present period of world politics and the postwar period of cold war, European union would still be advantageous to the United States. However, its benefits would not be those that most American opinion leaders have been anticipating. They expected that a united Europe would naturally conceive its interests and objectives in the world political and economic system in the same terms as the United States. In consequence, they believed that Atlantic partnership would be an effective means of mobilizing the resources and skills of North America and Western Europe for the achievement of the U.S. conception of a rational, peaceful and increasingly prosperous world order which, as explained in Chapter I, Americans assumed would be desired by all rational peace-loving nations.

Unrealistic as the American notion of Atlantic partnership may have been, there were during the 1950s and '60s and there are likely to be for the foreseeable future significant benefits for the United States in a united

Europe. As explained in the preceding chapter, the most powerful factor working toward European union is the desire to play an independent, active and important role in world politics. Such a development would probably mean even less European support for America's global objectives and policies than exists today. But, the attainment of superpower status by a united Europe would *ipso facto* relieve the United States of the substantial economic burden of European defense and of its feeling of responsibility for assuring European freedom and prosperity. Moreover, the very considerable narrowing, if not complete disappearance, of significant economic, military and other disparities between the United States and a united Europe would greatly enhance European self-confidence and sense of security. Alliances between equals are inclined to be less integrated and comprehensive than those dominated by a preponderant leader. Nevertheless, the changes in European attitudes likely to result from a closer approach to equality with the United States would make it less difficult to reach mutually satisfactory compromises on the specific economic and political conflicts of interest already existing and likely in the future to arise between a united Europe and the United States.

Thus, both subjectively and objectively, the declining prospects for European union adversely affect the present and prospective relationships between Western Europe and North America. If greater economic integration without decisive supranational unification is the most probable course of development for the EC, resolution of the specific economic and political issues between it and the United States will be more difficult.

In sum, the changing attitudes in the United States sketched in this chapter permeate considerations of national interest, obscuring the rational elements involved, exaggerating the importance of specific issues, and strengthening the resistances to mutually satisfactory compromises. By imparting a more nationalistic bias to American foreign policies and actions than was evident in the postwar years, they introduce new perplexities and uncertainties into transatlantic relationships and greatly complicate the task of responsible policy making on both sides of the Atlantic.

Canadian Attitudes in the Postwar Period

Over the past two and a half decades, Canadian attitudes and policies regarding European unification and the organization of the Atlantic region have reflected an increasingly complex variety of interests and problems and anxieties and expectations. They express not only the relevant aspects of Canada's economic and political relationships with other Atlantic countries — notably the United States and the United Kingdom — but also the profound internal changes within Canada that have become more and more evident in the course of the 1960s.

Compared with present complexities and perplexities, Canadian attitudes were fairly simple and straightforward in the early postwar years.

With less sense of responsibility for Europe's security and well-being than Americans, Canadians also were concerned about European defense and economic recovery during the late 1940s and early 1950s. Canada supported the ERP and favored European economic integration, although with much less missionary zeal than the United States. And, because its own security was at stake, Canada participated actively in the initiatives resulting in the establishment of NATO.

Canada's more restrained support of European integration reflected other considerations besides its lesser sense of responsibility for Europe's future. They arose from Canada's political ties and trade preferences in the Commonwealth and the ambivalence of its situation *vis-à-vis* the United States. Willingness of the United Kingdom to join the European unification movement at the beginning of the 1950s rather than a decade later would probably have evoked much more serious concern in Canada then than it did in the early 1960s. At that time, Canada's sense of closeness to the United Kingdom was greater, as were the relative benefits it then derived from participation in the Commonwealth's preferential trading system. Its relationship with the United Kingdom was still felt to be an effective counterpoise to its relationship with the United States. For, Canadians regarded their ties with the Commonwealth, and especially with the United Kingdom, as an anchor preventing them from being irresistibly drawn into the polity and economy of their enormous neighbor.

These concerns helped to shape Canadian attitudes toward the structure of the Atlantic region. An effectively organized regional system would assure Canadian security and more than replace the loss of preferential status in the British market by the much greater opportunities for the growth of trade in an integrated Atlantic system. Above all, Canadians would be able to enjoy the benefits of freer, if not free, access to the dynamic contiguous American market without the risk of being absorbed into the sovereignty of the United States. These considerations helped to generate considerable interest in Canada in Atlantic trade liberalization and proposals for regional free trade. They also contributed to Canadian willingness to participate actively in the successive rounds of tariff reductions in the GATT.

By the early 1960s, Canadian trade had grown substantially, its exports were beginning to shift toward industrial products, and the relative share of the United Kingdom in them was declining. Nonetheless, when in 1961 the United Kingdom initiated negotiations regarding membership in the EC, considerable concern was still felt in Canada. Certain major exports, such as cereals, pulp and paper, aluminium, lead and zinc, as well as the small but growing group of manufactured goods, were bound to be adversely affected by the loss of Canadian preferences in the British market coupled with the increased discrimination in favor of competing products from other full and associate members of the EC. Also, the possibility of British participation in the movement toward European union aroused Canadians' anxieties that they would be left alone with the United States. For these reasons, although Canadians were understanding of the factors that had impelled the United Kingdom to seek membership in the EC, they tended toward feelings of relief when General de Gaulle pronounced his veto.

Today, a decade later, Canadian reactions to the prospect of changes in the EC's membership are significantly different. For one thing, Canadians are much less interested in the probable economic effects, good and bad, of the enlargement of the EC; for another, they are even more concerned than a decade ago about the deep ambivalences in their relationships with the United States. These differences reflect important processes of change in the Canadian economy and more broadly within Canadian society as a whole, which may be briefly characterized.

Contemporary Changes in Canada and Their Effects on Attitudes toward Atlantic Relations

In the course of the decades since World War II, the Canadian economy has become increasingly industrialized. Among the major factors contributing to this development have been the inflows of U.S. capital, technology and managerial skills, in large part through the increasing number and size of the Canadian subsidiaries and branches of American business firms. In consequence, roughly half of Canadian manufacturing industry is now owned by American investors, as are important sectors of raw-material production and processing.

Another significant effect has been the changing composition and destination of Canadian trade. The United States has continued to be the largest market for Canadian exports, owing to its demand for Canadian raw materials, the transportation and other advantages of geographical proximity, and the fact that tariffs either do not exist or are quite low on a great many commodities traded between the two countries. Canadian industrialization has also meant that the proportion of manufactured goods in Canadian exports to the United States has been increasing, a process accelerated since 1965 by the agreement for free trade in automotive products. Whereas a decade ago roughly 12 percent of Canadian exports to the United States were manufactured goods, of which only 1/4 of one percent was automotive products, today the corresponding proportions are 48 percent and 31 percent.

In the course of the 1960s, Japan superseded Britain as Canada's second largest trading partner, and Canadian exports to it are increasing faster than to the United Kingdom. Moreover, Canada's trade with other countries in the Pacific, the Caribbean, the communist regions, and other parts of the world has been growing. Thus, although its exports to the United Kingdom and the EC are still substantial, they are relatively less important than a decade ago. However, the U.K. and West European markets retain their major significance for certain commodities, especially wheat, forest products and aluminium.

These shifts in the structure of the Canadian economy and in the composition and destination of its exports have contributed today to the lessening of apprehensions about the effects of the prospective enlargement of the EC. Not that Canadians are indifferent to it. Official concern has been expressed, and the producers likely to be most adversely affected are naturally worried. Nonetheless, the attention devoted to these issues by Canadian officials and opinion leaders is noticeably less now than in the past.

Canadian policy makers and economists are more concerned with the general implications of the development of the Canadian economy. Increasingly industrialized, it is correspondingly more dependent upon growing market demand, larger supplies of capital, continuous technological innovation, and rising managerial and labor skills. As explained in Chapter I, Atlantic economic integration provides comparatively small economies, such as Canada's, with access to these essential components of continued economic growth and increased living standards. Moreover, in important branches of Canadian industry, new plants are not likely to be established or existing factories expanded unless there is assured access to a larger market than that provided by Canada's own domestic demand. Some Canadian policy makers and economists believe that tariff reductions, like those agreed upon in the Kennedy Round, do not provide sufficient assurance; in their view, only binding commitments to free trade with the United States and other Atlantic countries would satisfy this requirement. In consequence, these Canadians have been interested in exploring the possibility of participating in free-trade arrangements.

For the reasons noted above, Canadians naturally regard the United States as the essential partner in any free-trade arrangement that would provide Canada with the benefits it needs. However, Canada's rising apprehensions over the substantial share of its industry now owned and managed by Americans have reinforced older anxieties about the danger of absorption into the United States. Hence, Canadians interested in free trade have sought the participation of other Atlantic countries not only to augment the positive benefits of the arrangement but also to serve as a counterpoise to the United States. These considerations would be likely to incline Canada favorably toward the possibilities for greater Atlantic economic integration discussed in Chapter IV.

Canadians' concern about their relations with the United States expresses not only the disproportionate nature of the economic interdependence between the two countries. It also reflects the profound process of sociocultural change which Canada, like other Atlantic countries, has been increasingly experiencing in the course of the 1960s. In general, it has the same characteristics and produces the same effects on attitudes and policies toward external relations as those described earlier in this chapter for the United States and in Chapter II for Western Europe. However, there are two aspects that are unique to Canada and importantly affect its relationships with other Atlantic nations.

One is the dramatic transformation of French Canadian self-conceptions and behavior. From a relatively static, inward-looking and essentially defensive society, French Canada (that is Quebec) has begun to experience major social changes that have already made it much more conscious of its cultural identity and intent upon achieving equality —economically, politically and socially— with English Canada. Some French Canadians are convinced that independence is a necessary precondition for realization of their potentialities; the majority, however, recognize the great benefits of continued participation in a united Canada. Initiatives from both groups are of increasing concern to other parts of Canada, as well as to the federal government in Ottawa. The pressures and resistances thereby engendered are difficult to contain, much less to resolve constructively. In recent years, this unique Canadian problem has been helping to divert Canadian attention and resources from foreign activities to domestic affairs.

The second aspect partly overlaps with the first. It consists of the dissatisfactions over the relationships among the different levels of Canada's political and administrative structure. They are expressed particularly in the disputes between the provincial governments, including Quebec, and the central government in Ottawa over the raising and dispensing of revenues, the relative responsibilities for determining priorities among social goals and the allocation of resources for achieving them, and the satisfaction of differing provincial needs and interests. These issues have also had the effect in recent years of focusing increased Canadian attention on internal problems.

The social conflicts arising from the fundamental process of socio-cultural change and its special Canadian manifestations have hitherto been less severe in Canada than in some other Atlantic countries, such as the United States, France and Italy. Nonetheless, they reinforce the effects of the economic developments noted above and of growing concern over the maintenance of Canadian sovereignty and cultural identity *vis-à-vis* the United States in concentrating the psychic energy and rational considera-tion of Canadians on domestic changes and problems. One consequence of Canada's increasingly inward focus is the declining interest in European affairs and lessened sense of responsibility for European security, as exemplified by the move to reduce Canadian commitments to NATO. Another is the more restrained reaction to the probable adverse economic effects of the prospective enlargement of the EC. However, Canada's relations with Western Europe are still recognized as of major importance even though they do not evoke at this time the deeply felt anxieties of previous years. And, many Canadians look to the future development of the Atlantic region as a whole as perhaps the most constructive way of maxi-mizing the benefits of Canada's relationships with the United States while minimizing the dangers they perceive for their economic and cultural independence.

IV The prospects for Transatlantic relations

In the course of the 1960s, a variety of economic and political issues have arisen in transatlantic relationships, some involving North Americans and Europeans generally, others specifically affecting the United States and the EC. To date, these problems have not been so serious as to impair the solidarity of the Atlantic region, which rests upon the basic sociocultural affinities of its component nations and their very extensive common interests. However, it is by no means certain that the factors hitherto responsible for Atlantic solidarity will continue to be stronger than the existing divisive issues and the new conflicts of interest bound to arise during the 1970s. For, the seriousness with which these specific economic and political problems are likely to be regarded depends not only upon their substantive importance *per se* but also on the more general attitudes and expectations of North Americans and Europeans with respect to the nature of transatlantic relationships. Accordingly, this chapter characterizes the main economic and political issues and explores the more and the less probable ways in which they would interact with the likely developments in Western Europe analyzed in Chapter II.

The Nature and Consequences of Atlantic Economic Difficulties

The existing and prospective economic issues between North America and Western Europe affect their trade, investment and monetary relationships. For our purposes, it is more important to understand what policy makers and opinion leaders on both sides of the Atlantic think about them than to determine whether or not their ideas and attitudes are verified by the facts.

The abolition of trade barriers within the EC and the coming into force of its common external tariff tend to be regarded in North America as increasing the relative discrimination against exports from Canada and the United States. Nor is the relative advantage for producers within the EC believed to be offset by the mutual reductions in the absolute levels of tariffs negotiated under the Kennedy Round. Further, it is felt that the admission of the United Kingdom and other European countries to the EC would additionally increase the scope of relative discrimination against North American exports. For their part, European producers and governments are disturbed by the failure of the United States to make certain changes in its tariff procedures agreed upon in the Kennedy Round and by the rising pressures from American business firms and trade unions for protection against imports.

While the growth of production by subsidiaries of American corporations in the EC has both contributed to and more than compensated for the actual and potential losses of U.S. exports of industrial products, no such development has been possible for certain North American agricultural commodities and semiprocessed materials, which constitute a substantial proportion of present and prospective exports from Canada and the United States to Western Europe. Especially important in this category are cereals, feedgrains, and oilseeds, which are already unfavorably affected by the common agricultural policy of the EC. British entry into the EC and the possibility of full or associate membership for the Scandinavian countries would have a further adverse effect on actual and potential exports of these commodities, as well as on Canadian exports of forest products.

Moreover, with the substantial absolute decline of tariff levels as a result of the successive rounds of tariff negotiations in the GATT, other types of discrimination in and distortion of trade have appeared to become comparatively more important on both sides of the Atlantic. They include border taxes of many kinds; product standards and health and sanitary regulations; discriminatory practices in government procurement; subsidies, tax incentives and other forms of aid to producers and regions within countries; preferential transportation and other charges; etc. In many cases adopted to serve purposes other than trade restriction, the discrimination and distortion resulting from these measures have hitherto been submerged in the much larger effects of tariffs and quantitative restrictions but are now being revealed by the reduction or abolition of the latter. Because of their multiplicity, unfamiliarity and primary justification by other national purposes, these nontariff barriers are difficult to reduce or eliminate, a characteristic that tends to intensify the resentment of exporters and governments adversely affected by them in North America and Western Europe.

As implied above, the changing nature of trade discrimination in the Atlantic region has been a major factor in stimulating the extraordinary growth of American direct investment in Western Europe since the late 1950s. This development has had ambivalent effects on both sides of the Atlantic. On the one hand, it has made a major contribution to European productivity, economic growth and living standards, and it has increased the earnings of American companies and thereby benefited the U.S. balance of payments. On the other hand, it has generated fear in Western Europe of American domination, and concern in the United States over the outflow of capital, the more rapid dissemination abroad of American technological advances, and the possible loss of jobs owing to forgone exports to and increased imports from Western Europe.

The trade and investment difficulties of the Atlantic region are important not only in themselves but also because they contribute to the monetary problems confronting North America and Western Europe. The monetary difficulties of the Atlantic region are complex and analysis of them is beyond the scope of this paper. Suffice it to say here, they are inherent in the nature of the existing international monetary system, in which the U.S. dollar plays a unique role as the predominant medium of commercial and financial transactions, a major form of reserve asset, and the standard for denominating the par values of other currencies. International monetary problems reflect the difficulties of mutual adjustment among national economies in an integrated regional economic system and the consequences of using the national currency of one of its members for international purposes. The results are substantial costs as well as benefits for all of the countries involved, including the United States, and deep ambivalences in interests and attitudes on both sides of the Atlantic.

Since existing monetary arrangements came into full operation with the restoration of current-account convertibility, these characteristics have led to a succession of international monetary crises. They have so far been successfully met by *ad hoc* emergency measures — mainly large short-term credits to support currencies under pressure — and by minimum structural reforms — principally the increase of liquidity through the establishment of special drawing rights — adopted only under the force of circumstances. The international monetary imbalances of several countries, notably of the United Kingdom and France on the deficit side and of Germany on the surplus side — have played important roles in these crises. However, the balance-of-payments deficit of the United States has been of central significance, both positively and negatively.

On the one hand, the net outflow of dollars from the United States has been and continues to be the source of most of the increased liquidity required to meet the needs of rising international trade and investment and the various national conceptions of desired levels of monetary reserves. In this sense, the U.S. balance-of-payments deficit is essential for maintaining the liquidity of the system and, therefore, confidence in its stability. But, on the other hand, the size and persistence of the U.S. deficit and the resulting uneasiness of many countries about accumulating and holding dollars in their monetary reserves have been and continue to be among the major reasons for the periodic weakening of confidence in the system and for discontent with its operation. The negative aspect is aggravated by the fact that the supply of dollars to the international system through the U.S. deficit is determined not only by the demand for them for international monetary purposes but also by the domestic economic conditions and policies of the United States and by its expenditures abroad for foreign policy purposes.

As a superpower with a strong sense of its world-transforming mission, the United States is unwilling to accept restraints on its international political and security policies to assuage the economic difficulties and anxieties of dollar-holding countries. It is especially reluctant to do so at the behest of prosperous European nations, which many Americans believe are shirking their responsibilities for helping to preserve world peace and freedom and even for meeting the costs of their own defense. In a democratic society whose people are intent upon transforming their unrivaled productivity into ever-rising living standards and more equitable distribution of income, the U.S. government is unable to impose the kinds of restrictions on its own budgetary expenditures and on the American economy as a whole that could maintain the balance of payments in reasonable equilibrium. For their part, the Europeans are unwilling to support indirectly, through the accumulation of dollars, U.S. foreign policies over which they have very little influence and which they regard as being unrealistic and dangerous. And, in similarly democratic societies whose people are equally determined to realize the fruits of their own unprecedented productivity, European governments are also unable to ignore the consequences for their domestic economic conditions of the imbalances and crises of confidence of the international monetary system.

Despite their seriousness, the economic difficulties besetting the Atlantic region have hitherto been met by efforts to preserve the substantial degree of economic interdependence and integration already achieved. Instead of splitting the region into two parts or deteriorating into neomercantilism, as during the 1930s, the crises produced by the tensions between the fundamental trends within and among Atlantic countries have so far been dealt with by closer intergovernmental cooperation and slowly growing coordination of national economic policies, larger emergency credits and other forms of mutual assistance, and the establishment of a new international reserve asset, the SDRs. Before analyzing the factors determining whether or not the integrative forces in the regional system will continue to prevail over the disintegrative tendencies, it is necessary to consider briefly the political and military aspects of the transatlantic relationship.

Political and Military Difficulties of the Atlantic Region

In contrast to the economic aspects, the trend of political-military relationships in the course of the 1960s has been toward looser, less integrated ties. This difference reflects the changing nature of the national attitudes and interests involved and the varying degrees of adequacy of the Atlantic system for expressing or advancing them.

As explained earlier, the expectation of many Americans and some Europeans proved to be fruitless that an Atlantic partnership would evolve to assure the security of the Atlantic region and to mobilize its energies and resources for managing Atlantic participation in the world political system. The proposals for greater military integration among NATO members, as expressed particularly in the Multilateral Force (MLF) scheme, foundered and were tacitly abandoned by the United States. The withdrawal of French forces from the integrated NATO command and the subsequent shift, at France's request, of NATO headquarters from Paris to Brussels further discouraged the movement for Atlantic military-political integration. European dissatisfaction with American political leadership intensified after the mid-1960s, when U.S. involvement in the Indochina war escalated, and frustrated American efforts to conduct a world political strategy with the united and active support of its NATO allies. The United Kingdom's gradual reduction of responsibilities "east of Suez" reinforced this trend in the late 1960s. Thus, by the end of the decade, it became clear that the political and military difficulties of NATO were being resolved by moving away from instead of toward greater political and military integration of the Atlantic region.

With respect to the worldwide military and political interests of the Atlantic countries, the changes in the international system noted in Chapter II have been decisive. The decline both of the direct Soviet menace to Western Europe and of the threat that recurrent political crises in other parts of the world would trigger a nuclear war between the superpowers has raised serious questions in Canada and the European members of NATO about the need for even the existing degree of military integration and political coordination among Atlantic countries. In their view, the functions that NATO will have to perform in the prospective world political situation do not require the kind of political and military integration that seemed essential — and was sought — during the postwar period of cold war. They tend more and more to see the persisting external dangers necessitating continuation of NATO as being threats only to the Atlantic region in the strict geographical sense of the term, in contrast to the American conception of the global scope of Atlantic security and political interests and hence of the obligations of its NATO allies to support its activities elsewhere in the world.

So far, none of the changes in the international system as a whole and in the Atlantic region has seriously shaken the conviction of the European members that their security requires continued reliance upon the U.S. nuclear deterrent and on the apparent willingness of the United States to use it, as well as its conventional forces, in their defense. Nor are European attitudes and military capabilities likely to change sufficiently in the next decade or so for them voluntarily to dispense with the American commitment to protect them explicitly against the Russians and implicitly against the Germans, or any other European nation seeking to rule the continent against its will. For its part, the United States will in all probability continue to believe that it cannot allow the human capabilities, productive resources and military potential of Western Europe to be dominated by any superpower, or even prospective superpower, likely to use them against North America or to attack American interests in other regions of the world. These considerations define the limits of the continuing common Atlantic interest in the preservation of an alliance — presumably NATO.

Beyond them, however, attitudes and interests on opposite sides of the Atlantic have been diverging in the course of the 1960s and will do so in the foreseeable future. On the one hand, the sense of America's world-transforming mission, the activism and self-confidence inherent in its faith in the efficacy of technocratic prescriptions, and the desire to preserve its paramount superpower status reinforce the mutual suspicion and competition of its relations with the Soviet Union in continuing to impel the United States to a global conception of its interests and responsibilities. On the other hand, the restored adequacy and continued institutional strengthening of European nation-states, the increasing technocratic activism and slowly reviving senses of mission of their own elites, and the self-confidence engendered both by these developments and, paradoxically, by the progress hitherto made in unifying Europe all combine to foster the tendency to repudiate American leadership and direction and more and more to insist on determining their own goals and priorities, internally and externally.

In the light of these common and conflicting interests and attitudes, the most probable course of development is that NATO would continue to be a conventional type of alliance. In it, national military forces would be sufficiently coordinated — through a unified command structure and defensive doctrine more or less determined by its nuclear superpower member, the United States — to constitute a minimum credible arrangement for dealing with the probable external and internal threats to European security and independence. That the alliance would be minimal in functions and degree of integration — as, in fact, it has already become — is dictated by the political and sociocultural constraints and not by economic inadequacies or by inability to devise more appropriate military doctrines and conditions of preparedness. The United States will probably continue to try to improve NATO's combat effectiveness and its strategy and tactics for meeting the various possible contingencies that might confront the alliance in Europe. But, regardless of the strictly military considerations involved, these efforts will generally be doomed to failure insofar as they require significantly greater impairment either of European or of American freedom of action than now exists.

Effects of the Enlargement of the EC

It is only in the broader context of Europe's fundamental structure that the most significant consequences of the addition of new members to the EC can be assessed.

Persisting confidence on both sides of the Atlantic that the entry of the United Kingdom, Denmark, Ireland and Norway into the EC as full members would foster — or at least not inhibit — the unification movement would be conducive to continuing containment of specific economic and political differences between North America and Western Europe. However, as Chapter II has explained, the enlargement of the EC is more likely to diminish rather than increase the probability that the crucial fiscal and monetary powers will be transferred to supranational authorities in the foreseeable future. As this development becomes manifest, it would have the adverse consequences on both American and European attitudes explained in preceding chapters.

In addition, there are other ways in which the enlargement of the EC and the form in which it is accomplished would exacerbate the economic and political issues and thereby worsen transatlantic relationships. The inclusion of the United Kingdom and some of the other EFTA members within the EC's external tariff and common agricultural policy would automatically increase the relative discrimination against North American exports generally and the absolute barriers against agricultural products. Dissatisfactions in North America over these developments would be magnified by the greater relative importance now attached to nontariff forms of preferential treatment for producers within the EC compared with North American exporters.

The adverse reaction in North America to such developments would be compounded if the enlargement of the EC were to be accomplished through associate, rather than full, membership for the United Kingdom and possibly other countries. The United States has become increasingly concerned over the widening circle of countries in Europe, the Near East and Africa that have preferential trade arrangements with the EC, and over the proposals that others in these regions be accorded similar status. North Americans are already tending to regard the EC as a growing preferential trade bloc which threatens not only their own trade but also that of developing countries in Latin America and Asia. Associate membership for the United Kingdom and other European countries (i.e., sooner or later and in one form or another, Austria, Denmark, Finland, Iceland, Ireland, Portugal, Spain, Sweden and Switzerland) would more than confirm this fear in American and Canadian minds. By further sapping their faith in the likelihood of European union, such a development would additionally magnify the seriousness of transatlantic economic and political conflicts.

Finally, even if the United Kingdom and other European countries were to join the EC as full members, this development would tend to polarize the Atlantic region and to sharpen the specific economic and political issues between the two parts. Hitherto, the EFTA — especially its largest member, the United Kingdom — has to a significant extent acted as a buffer between the EC and the United States, somewhat complicating the economic problems of the region but thereby also diffusing the issues and constraining them from provoking disintegrative conflicts. The disappearance of this mediating function would undoubtedly be regarded by Americans as a small loss to be borne for the benefits to Atlantic relations of European union. But, as the declining likelihood of European union becomes increasingly apparent, the effects of the bipolarity and sharpening of issues within the Atlantic region will be more and more divisive.

In sum, if enlargement of the EC by the entry of the United Kingdom and other European countries as full members were, as seems likely, to diminish the prospects for European union, the specific economic and political issues would be regarded by Americans as much more serious. Europeans would also tend to take them more seriously in the absence of the unity that would enable them to deal more nearly as equals with the United States. Hence, transatlantic conflicts would be intensified. And, if the United Kingdom and others were to join as associate members, the resulting reaction in North America would significantly increase the likelihood of the disintegration of the Atlantic economic system.

The More and Less Probable Developments in Atlantic Relations

Basic to the solidarity of the Atlantic regional system is the fact that all of its constituent nation-states are descendants of the historical Western civilization and constitute those contemporary forms of Western society and culture that have the greatest similarities in institutional systems, values and behavioral norms. These fundamental affinities tend to be taken for granted and hence their importance as factors shaping the future of transatlantic relations is discounted. For this reason, it is necessary to stress that, of all the ties that bind the Atlantic nations together, those comprised in their common sociocultural heritage are the most pervasive and among the most powerful. Despite evident and significant differences, the people of the Atlantic countries feel, see, believe, think and act more like one another than like the people of those other contemporary descendants of Western civilization in the communist states of Eastern Europe and in the modernizing nations of Latin America. Their societies and cultures are certainly much more similar to one another than to the non-Western transitional societies and cultures of Asia and Africa. And, in the new period of international relations, when for the first time world politics has become truly global and all countries participate in it as more or less significant actors and no longer as mere spectators or helpless prizes, the importance of basic sociocultural similarities and differences is and will continue to be manifested in many unpredictable ways.

As explained in Chapter I, all of the economic — and some of the political and psychological — problems of transatlantic relationships are specific forms of the general process of continuous mutual adjustment among national economies in an integrated regional system, one of whose members is of disproportionate size and plays a unique role in its economic functioning. These difficulties of competition and adjustment are intensified and their resolution made more difficult by the tensions between two opposing trends:

1. To achieve and preserve the regional economic integration needed to foster their economic growth, the Atlantic nations have voluntarily committed themselves not to exercise certain sovereign powers over their external trade and payments — powers by which, in the past, they were accustomed to insulate their national economic systems as a whole, or sectors or branches within them, from undesired external influences.
2. At the same time as they have been forgoing use of these important instruments of economic policy, national governments have been acquiring the new and more difficult functions and responsibilities that impel them to greater and more effective management of their own economic systems at *macro* and *micro* levels.

These trends are important because they define both the limits of the probable realities within which policy makers will have to cope with specific problems and the kinds of policy measures available to them.

The extremes of the possible range within which these trends could develop are:

- At the one end, the disintegration of the Atlantic economic system, most likely along the major potential line of cleavage running through the Atlantic ocean. This would resolve the tensions by restoring full control over their *macro* and *micro* management policies, on the one side, to the United States and those countries, such as Canada, voluntarily or perforce associated with it; and, on the other side, to the EC and those EFTA members willing and able to join it in a larger and probably more integrated European arrangement.
- At the other end, complete economic integration of the Atlantic region as a whole. This would resolve the tensions by allowing much greater scope for market forces to harmonize national economic conditions and narrow the disparities among member countries. But, it would require the establishment of a supranational Atlantic authority to enforce the coordination of fiscal, monetary and regulatory policies needed to ensure that income and employment expectations would be met, reasonable price stability maintained, and unacceptable hardships and disparities in different parts of the region mitigated.

The latter extreme — that, in effect, the Atlantic region would form an economic and political union — has by far the smallest probability. It is difficult to imagine developments that could so impair the American sense of the adequacy of its nation-state as to make the United States willing to join an Atlantic union, in which its influence would not be paramount and its freedom of action would be correspondingly restricted. Even an arrangement by which the European countries would accede to the existing federal union of the United States would probably be bitterly resisted by large sections of American elite-group and public opinion and might not be approved by the Congress. Conversely, any kind of Atlantic federation in which the United States would be predominant would be regarded by most Europeans as an American empire, not as a union of equals, and they would be unlikely to join it voluntarily. Only an external menace of such magnitude and imminence as to make the alternatives of uniting or perishing unequivocally the only choices would be likely to overcome these serious obstacles on both sides to an Atlantic union. And, this development is among the least probable of the foreseeable future.

The other possible extreme of the range — the disintegration of the Atlantic region into European and North American groupings — has a much higher probability. Indeed, judged solely in the light of present attitudes and conflicts, it could be the most probable development. Viewed in the longer-term perspective of basic sociocultural affinities and continuing common economic and political interests, however, it is not.

The most likely way in which the disintegrative possibility could become reality would be through a vicious spiral of mutual restrictions and retaliations. In other words, disintegration of the Atlantic region would probably not be the result of a single explicit decision on either side but rather the outcome of an extended process of worsening relations and deepening resentments. Nor would it make much difference which specific aspect of growing economic difficulties were to trigger the process, because all would be likely to help sustain it.

With respect to trade relations, actions of the EC — or its refusal to act — could intensify the already evident American suspicion that it was becoming nothing more than an expanding preferential trading arrangement adverse to the interests of the United States and other countries against which it was discriminating. In such circumstances, the United States, Canada, Japan and other excluded nations could be impelled to form a preferential trading arrangement of their own — just as the EFTA was established by the European countries unwilling or unable to join the EC at its inception. Or, tariffs and quantitative restrictions reimposed by the United States in response to pressures from American business firms and trade unions could induce the EC to adopt compensatory restrictions of its own, which could precipitate a chain of retaliatory measures by each side. Increased competition in third markets between European and North American exporters could generate charges of dumping and other unfair trade practices, as has happened already with respect to both U.S. and EC efforts to dispose of their respective surplus agricultural commodities. Such developments would at the least exacerbate resentments on both sides of the Atlantic and at the worst could set off increasingly serious trade wars.

The vicious spiral could be initiated or reinforced by developments primarily affecting investment relationships. Broader or more uncompromising application of the extraterritoriality principle by the United States could strengthen European fears that the subsidiaries of large American corporations were in fact 'Trojan horses' for subjugating their national economies to American control. Conversely, increased regulation of American subsidiaries by European governments or real or imagined discriminatory treatment of them could generate more and more bitter controversies between the United States and the EC. Another source of contention could be the adverse effects on European capital markets of restrictions that might be imposed by the U.S government on the export of American capital in response to the concern of trade unions and others over the real or suspected loss of employment resulting from production abroad by U.S. firms.

Similarly, the vicious spiral could be started or greatly intensified by developments in monetary relationships. Persisting large U.S. balance-of-payments deficits could so alarm European monetary authorities that they would refuse to accumulate additional dollars in their reserves. In such circumstances, European governments could feel impelled to cut their currencies loose from the dollar. Two currency blocs would in effect be created, having fluctuating exchange rates between them or restrictions on their mutual trade and capital flows. The likelihood of such a monetary split would certainly be increased by European fears that the U.S. payments deficit was forcing them to 'import inflation' or to support U.S. foreign policies to which they were opposed.

Regardless of the specific problems and disputes that might initiate and sustain this vicious spiral, its momentum would be increased by the more general attitudinal and institutional factors discussed in the two preceding sections. American disillusionment and European frustration over the waning prospects for European union would incline both sides to take the specific issues much more seriously. For, the actions generating such responses would no longer be regarded as means to a mutually desired goal but as ends in themselves, whose adverse consequences would not be more than offset by future benefits. Moreover, as explained earlier, the bipolarization of the Atlantic region resulting from enlargement of the EC would tend to sharpen the issues between North America and Western Europe. True, as many Americans and Britons believe —and as General de Gaulle objected— the United Kingdom's influence in the EC would probably be exerted to moderate disputes and facilitate compromises between the two sides, and to foster more liberal trade policies. But, much, if not all, of the effectiveness of this positive factor would be lost if the United Kingdom were to join the EC as an associate, rather than a full, member. Indeed, such an event could itself trigger the vicious spiral and would certainly strengthen it substantially if it were already underway.

Britain's influence as a full member of the EC would be important in inhibiting the tendencies toward disintegration of the Atlantic region. However, the most powerful factors counteracting such a development are the common economic and political interests served by Atlantic economic integration and the U.S. nuclear guarantee of European security and freedom; the self-reinforcing momentum of the institutions and relationships that have already developed to realize these interests; and the pervasive cohesion engendered by the basic sociocultural affinities. Moreover, these positive factors support and increase Atlantic solidarity not only separately but also by strengthening one another. The basic sociocultural affinities predispose the Atlantic nations to look to one another for mutual protection and assistance and to trust the commitments made pursuant to these common concerns. The pressures generated by the existing high degree of economic integration for closer harmonization of national economic conditions and greater coordination of national economic policies also operate to narrow the disparities in capabilities and attitudes and thereby to strengthen the sociocultural affinities. The common interest in meeting the minimum mutual defense need magnifies the importance of continued economic integration beyond the economic benefits derived therefrom. The continuation of economic integration reinforces the military capabilities and political solidarity of the alliance. In these and other ways, the positive sociocultural, political-military and economic factors are mutually supporting; indeed, they are only conceptually distinguishable aspects of a complex of relationships that so interpenetrate one another as to constitute a seamless web of durable ties.

Thus, in the long-term perspective of basic affinities and common interests, it is significantly less probable that specific problems and conflicts will disintegrate the Atlantic region than that they will not. If this evaluation is valid, it means that Atlantic relationships are most likely to continue to develop in the middle portion of the range between Atlantic union at one extreme and the splitting of the region into competing blocs at the other. Moreover, it means that decisions of political leaders and policy makers and the extent of popular support for them will be of major importance in determining how close to either extreme the actual course of events will be. The closer developments are to either end of the range, the greater the probability that the outcome will resemble one or the other extreme. Thus, because the extreme of disintegration of the region has a substantially higher probability than the extreme of Atlantic union, policy choices and actions tending toward the former would still further increase its likelihood.

Some Implications for Policy

For this reason, a brief analysis needs to be made of the ways in which policy decisions would affect these relative probabilities. Two kinds of policy approaches can be distinguished for dealing with the difficulties and dangers in transatlantic relationships during the 1970s.

The first would handle each issue as it occurs, considering it in its own terms, and endeavoring to negotiate an acceptable compromise between the interests involved, or a package of compromises covering several simultaneous problems. However, because this *ad hoc* approach treats symptoms and not causes, new difficulties would continually arise. The repeated exacerbation of feelings on both sides would correspondingly increase the danger of provoking the vicious spiral of restrictions and retaliations and would raise the related probability of the disintegrative exteme of possible future Atlantic relationships.

In contrast, the alternative approach would endeavor to mitigate the underlying pressures from which the specific problems arise. Removing them completely would, of course, require the full economic and political unification of the Atlantic region which, as explained above, has a very low probability. But, there are steps that can be taken well short of full union which could reduce the underlying tensions sufficiently to eliminate many of the symptomatic problems, as well as benefit both sides of the transatlantic relationship in positive ways.

Within the more probable middle range of possible developments, the most effective form of the second approach would be a free-trade arrangement among the Atlantic nations and Japan and including countries elsewhere in the world willing and able to join it. Although initially the pressures generated by *macro* adjustments among national economies and by more intense *micro* competition would increase, the beneficial effects of free trade and capital movements will in time reduce them substantially. For, in addition to stimulating economic growth, free trade also hastens the narrowing of disparities among participating countries in wages, prices, living standards, etc. Even with the existing degree of Atlantic economic integration, competitive pressures and cooperative arrangements among business firms of different nationalities are already fostering greater technological research and faster dissemination of the results, stimulating more innovative attitudes and efficient managerial methods, and continually redistributing comparative advantages and disadvantages within the region.

A free-trade arrangement would constrain member countries to use better means than tariffs and payment barriers for counteracting adverse effects on employment and incomes and for assisting business firms, workers and farmers to adjust to increased competition. Such means include three types of coordinated actions among participating governments: (1) harmonization of those elements of their national fiscal and monetary policies that help to generate excessively disruptive movements of goods and money among the member countries; (2) abolition or equalization of the nontariff forms of discrimination and trade distortion that importantly affect the conditions of competition; and (3) coordination of programs of adjustment assistance to individual business firms, workers and farmers, of plans for developing backward or declining regions within countries, of industrial development policies, and of measures for preserving portions of noncompetitive branches of industry and agriculture for defense or sociopolitical reasons.

Chapter II has explained that the necessary concerting of these national economic policies and programs can be effectuated through cooperation of the governments concerned, and does not require supranational authority. The fact that free trade without supranational authority is feasible means that objections to such an institutional development would not prevent formation of this type of integrated arrangement, as they would a full economic union among Atlantic countries. Nonetheless, there would be other serious obstacles to a proposal for a free-trade arrangement. In addition to the fears of business firms, workers and farmers concerned about the adverse effects of free trade, it would encounter the formidable difficulty of the EC's unwillingness to abolish its common external tariff and to revise drastically its common agricultural policy.

These two devices now provide the major immediate economic incentives holding the EC together. Substantial progress in transferring the crucial fiscal and monetary powers to the supranational authority would enable the EC to dispense with the common external tariff and common agricultural policy without endangering its continued existence. However, as explained in Chapter II, greater economic integration will more probably occur in the EC without significant augmentation of supranational authority. Instead, it would be accomplished through the adoption of additional common policies and more effective cooperation among member governments. Such measures of further economic integration could also substitute in greater or lesser part for the common external tariff in holding the EC together. Also, in either case, the financial burden of the common agricultural policy and the long-term economic and demographic trends affecting European farming are bound to lead sooner or later to its drastic revision.

Hence, over time, it is possible that the EC's members would come to believe that the benefits of joining a larger free-trade arrangement could be obtained without risking the EC's cohesiveness by abolishing its common external tariff and modifying its agricultural policy. Moreover, in these circumstances, not only institutional momentum but also political and psychological considerations would help to keep the EC alive. For, in a free-trade arrangement, the organization would constitute a 'united front' *vis-à-vis* the United States that would foster European self-confidence and negotiating effectiveness through the cumulated economic resources it represented and the combined experience and skills it embodied.

On balance, then, it must be concluded that, although a free-trade arrangement would be the most effective means for dealing with the divisive threat to the Atlantic region, the probability of its adoption is significantly greater in the longer term — say in the second half of the 1970s — than in the shorter term. This means, in effect, that free trade is more likely to be the end product of growing Atlantic economic integration than it is to be the starting point. For, without any further trade liberalization than that already agreed upon in the Kennedy Round, the Atlantic countries would still be able to maintain and strengthen their economic integration in other ways. Some or all of the coordinated policies and programs characterized in (1), (2) and (3) above could be undertaken without free trade. Other measures fostering Atlantic integration that could be adopted include further improvements in the liquidity and flexibility of the international monetary system and more frequent and constructive multilateral consultations prior to making important changes in national fiscal and monetary policies. As explained above, these means of achieving greater Atlantic economic integration would be essential elements of a free-trade arrangement. But, alternatively, they could be adopted independently of free trade and would pave the way for it, even though they would not be as effective in relieving the underlying pressures and, therefore, in reducing the symptomatic problems.

This sketch of the alternatives for a creative approach to the divisive threats confronting the Atlantic regional system indicates that it is by nature more difficult than the *ad hoc* approach and requires more statesmanlike leadership on both sides of the Atlantic. Nonetheless, there is a substantial probability that the continuing frustrations and dangers inherent in the *ad hoc* approach will sooner or later provide the necessary incentives to Atlantic statesmen to choose one or the other constructive alternative. This probability is enhanced by the fact that the self-reinforcing momentum inherent in the economic integration process — while by no means as irresistible as envisaged in the theory of functional inevitability —

will be a powerful positive force operating to broaden and deepen the Atlantic regional integration already achieved at both governmental and private levels.

In sum, the course of development likely to ensue under the creative approach would not be a panacea for the problems of the Atlantic region. The nature of these difficulties is such as to make their complete removal unlikely because the means for doing so will continue to be politically unacceptable to both sides. But, neither is it more probable that the issues would be so magnified as to precipitate the splitting of the region. Thus, the Atlantic system will continue to be plagued by serious economic issues, political difficulties, and psychological anxieties and frustrations which, even if they cannot be resolved, will at least be prevented from fatally undermining the security, prosperity and dynamism of its member nations.

The parallel processes of increasing European and Atlantic economic integration — in part competitive and in part mutually supportive — would involve progressive restrictions on the freedom of action of national governments. Such a trend would mean that, along with the strengthening of the domestic institutional bases of Atlantic nation-states, their scope for conducting independent economic policies and actions would be narrowing. In effect, they would be exercising their sovereign economic powers more and more in common. This process differs sufficiently in its organizational and operational manifestations from the deliberate transfer of crucial economic functions to supranational authorities for it to be much more acceptable politically and psychologically to both North Americans and Europeans. Thus, while the institutional roots of nation-states would continue to spread wider and deeper within their own societies, their branches would grow more and more intertwined and interdependent.

This course of development would not be likely in the foreseeable future to lead to the formal merger of sovereignty in an Atlantic federation, for the reasons explained above. But, if the trend continues for the remainder of the century, it could well be that new forms of large-scale social organization would imperceptibly evolve at both Atlantic and European levels that, in accordance with the paradoxical nature of human history, would in quite unintended and unexpected ways both preserve the diversity and strengthen the unity of the region. Such developments would mark the end of the current period of the new nationalism, at least for the Atlantic countries. Whether and in what circumstances the independent sovereign nation-state might in this manner eventually pass away are speculative questions whose determinants within Atlantic societies and in the regional and worldwide systems lie beyond the range for which a projective analysis can validly be made. Nonetheless, it is probable that, for all their continuing tensions and problems — indeed, in part because of them — Western society and culture will still be capable of great creative acts of innovation and statesmanship when the times are again propitious for them.

Members of the British-North American Committee

Co-Chairmen:

LORD HOWICK
Chairman, Commonwealth Development Corporation
London

HAROLD SWEATT
Honorary Chairman of the Board, Honeywell Inc.
Minneapolis, Minnesota

Chairman, Executive Committee

ROBERT M. FOWLER
President, Canadian Pulp and Paper Association
Montreal, Quebec

Members

A. E. BALLOCH
President, Bowater's Canadian Corporation Ltd
Montreal, Quebec

DAVID BARRAN
Chairman, Shell Transport and Trading Company Ltd
London

LEONARD BEATON
London

PETER BESSELL
London

JAMES H. BINGER
Chairman of the Board, Honeywell Inc.
Minneapolis, Minnesota

WILLIAM S. BREWSTER
Chairman of the Board, USM Corporation
Boston, Massachusetts

HARRY BRIDGES
President, Shell Canada Ltd
Toronto, Ontario

LLEWELLYN L. CALLAWAY, JR.
Vice-Chairman, *Newsweek*, Inc.
New York, New York

LESLIE CANNON
General President, Electrical, Electronic, Telecommunication Union/Plumbing Trades Union
London

DR. CHARLES CARTER
Vice-Chancellor, University of Lancaster
Lancashire

H. F. R. CATHERWOOD
Director-General, National Economic Development Council
London

FRANCOIS E. CLEYN
Chairman of the Board and Chief Executive Officer, Cleyn & Tinker Ltd
Huntingdon, Quebec

HON. J. V. CLYNE
Chairman and Chief Executive Officer, MacMillan Bloedel Ltd
Vancouver, British Columbia

LORD COLLISON
London

JAMES CONWAY
General Secretary, Amalgamated Union of Engineering and Foundry Workers
London

LORD COOPER
General Secretary, General and Municipal Workers Union
Esher, Surrey

C. L. S. COPE
Overseas Director, Confederation of British Industry
London

JOHN S. DICKEY
President Emeritus and Professor of Public Affairs, Dartmouth College, New Hampshire

WILLIAM DODGE
Secretary-Treasurer, Canadian Labour Congress
Ottawa, Ontario

SIR ERIC DRAKE
Chairman, The British Petroleum Co, Ltd
London

DOUGLAS R. FULLER
President, The Northern Trust Company
Chicago, Illinois

GEORGE GOYDER
Chairman, British International Paper Ltd
London

AUGUSTIN S. HART
Executive Vice-President, Quaker Oats Company
Chicago, Illinois

HENRY J. HEINZ II
Chairman of the Board, H. J. Heinz Company
Pittsburg, Pennsylvania

JAMES H. INGERSOLL
Vice President-International, Borg-Warner Corporation
Chicago Illinois

HARRY G. JOHNSON
Professor of Economics, London School of Economics and Political Science, and University of Chicago

JOSEPH D. KEENAN
International Secretary, International Brotherhood of Electrical Workers, AFL-CIO
Washington, D.C.

TOM KILLEFER
Vice President-Finance and General Counsel,
Chrysler Corporation
Detroit, Michigan

WILLIAM LADYMAN
International Vice-President, International
Brotherhood of Electrical Workers, AFL-CIO-CLC
Toronto, Ontario

R. STANLEY LAING
President, The National Cash Register Company
Dayton, Ohio

HERBERT H. LANK
Director, Du Pont of Canada Ltd
Montreal, Quebec

FRANKLIN A. LINDSAY
President, Itek Corporation
Lexington, Massachusetts

DONALD MacDONALD
President, Canadian Labour Congress
Ottawa, Ontario

RAY W. MACDONALD
President, Burroughs Corporation
Detroit, Michigan

JOHN G. McLEAN
President, Continental Oil Company
New York, New York

PETER MENZIES
Deputy Chairman, Imperial Chemical Industries Ltd
London

J. IRWIN MILLER
Chairman of the Board,
Cummins Engine Company, Inc.
Columbus, Indiana

DEREK F. MITCHELL
President, B.P. Canada Ltd
Montreal, Quebec

DR. MALCOLM MOOS
President, University of Minnesota
Minneapolis, Minnesota

CHARLES MUNRO
President, Canadian Federation of Agriculture
Ottawa, Ontario

KENNETH D. NADEN
Executive Vice-President, National Council of
Farmer Co-operatives
Washington, D.C.

FREDERICK E. NOLTING, JR.
Assistant to the Chairman
Morgan Guaranty Trust Company
New York, New York

GENERAL LAURIS NORSTAD
Chairman of the Board,
Owens-Corning Fiberglas Corporation
Toledo, Ohio

SIR MAURICE PARSONS
Chairman, The Bank of London and
South America Ltd
London

SIR DENNING PEARSON
Chairman and Chief Executive, Rolls-Royce Ltd
Derby, Derbyshire

DAVID POWELL
Chairman, Booker McConnell & Company, Ltd
London

J. G. PRENTICE
Chairman, Canadian Forest Products Ltd
Vancouver, British Columbia

SIR DEREK PRITCHARD
Chairman, Allied Breweries Ltd
London

GEORGE E. PUTNAM, JR.
Senior Vice-President, First National City Bank
New York, New York

J. MARTIN RITCHIE
Chairman, The Bowater Paper Corporation Ltd
London

V. E. ROCKHILL
Chairman, Chase Manhattan Overseas Banking
Corporation
New York, New York

HOWARD I. ROSS
Dean of Faculty of Management, McGill University
Montreal, Quebec

A. C. I. SAMUEL
Group Overseas Co-ordinator,
Constructors John Brown Ltd
London

LAURENCE P. SCOTT
Chairman, The Manchester Guardian and
Evening News Ltd
Manchester.

SIR FREDERIC SEEBOHM
Chairman, Barclays Bank D.C.O.
London

THE EARL OF SELKIRK
President, Royal Central Asian Society
London

LORD SHERFIELD
Chairman, Industrial and Commercial Finance
Corporation
London

G. F. SMITH
General Secretary, Amalgamated Society of
Woodworkers
London

LEROY D. SMITHERS
President, Dow Chemical of Canada, Ltd
Sarnia, Ontario

CHARLES SOLOMON
President, Mobil International Oil Company
New York, New York

LAUREN K. SOTH
Editor of the Editorial Pages,
Des Moines Register & Tribune
Des Moines, Iowa

DR. J. E. WALLACE STERLING
Chancellor, Stanford University
California

RALPH I. STRAUS
Director, R. H. Macy & Company, Inc.
New York, New York

Sponsoring Organisations

The British-North American Research Association was inaugurated in December 1969 with the primary purpose of sponsoring the research work, and providing an administrative framework for, the British members of the British-North American Committee. The Association is recognised as a Charity and is governed by an executive committee of British members of the British-North American Committee under the chairmanship of Lord Howick. It will sponsor and publish research into the developing relationship between Britain and North America.

The Association's office is at 12 Upper Belgrave Street, London SW1 (Tel. 01-235 1833).

The National Planning Association was founded in 1934 as an independent, private, non-profit, and non-political organisation. It engages in studies and develops recommendations based on non-partisan research or analysis on major policy issues confronting the United States, both in domestic affairs and in international relations. Its research provides information and methodologies valuable to public and private decision makers.

NPA is governed by a Board of Trustees representing all private sectors of the American economy — business, labour, farm, and the professions. The Steering Committee of the Board, the four Standing Committees (the Agriculture, Business, and Labour Committees on National Policy, and the Committee on International Policy), and Special Policy Committees (including the British-North American Committee) originate and approve policy statements and reports. Major research projects undertaken for government and international agencies, and through foundation grants, are carried out with the guidance of research advisory committees providing the best knowledge available. The full-time staff of the Association as of 1 January 1970 totalled around seventy professional and administrative personnel.

The Association has a public membership of some 3,000 individuals, corporations, organisations and groups. NPA activities are financed by contributions from individuals, business firms, trade unions, and farm organisations; by grants for specific research projects from private foundations; and by research contracts with Federal, state, and local government agencies and international organisations.

NPA publications, including those of the British-North American Committee, can be obtained from the Association's office, 1606 New Hampshire Avenue, NW, Washington, DC, 20009 (Tel. 202-265-7685).

The Private Planning Association of Canada is a private, non-political, non-profit organisation created in 1958 for the purpose of undertaking independent and objective studies of Canadian problems and policies, mainly in the fields of economic affairs and of Canada's international relationships with other countries.

The Association is sponsored by a large number of private donors, including business firms, labour unions, and agricultural federations, who make annual financial contributions in support of its work. Specific study projects and programmes have, from time to time, also received assistance from foundations and from Federal and provincial government agencies.

A large part of the work of the Association is carried on under the auspices of Committees, composed of agricultural, business, educational, labour, and professional leaders who meet to consider important national issues and to sponsor and review studies that contribute to better public understanding of such issues. At present there are three such Committees: the Canadian-American Committee, founded in 1957 and sponsored jointly by the National Planning Association in Washington, DC; the Canadian Economic Policy Committee, formed in 1969 by expansion of the terms of reference of the former Canadian Trade Committee; and the newly founded British-North American Committee, sponsored jointly with the National Planning Association and the British-North American Research Association.

PPAC publications are available from the Association's office, 2060 Sun Life Building, Montreal 110, Quebec (Tel. 514-861-6319).

Publications of the British-North American Committee

An overall view of international economic questions facing Britain, the United States, and Canada during the 1970's
by Harry G. Johnson, June, 1970, price 8s. (40 n.p.) $1.00 BN-1

Transatlantic relations in the prospect of an enlarged European Community
by Theodore Geiger, November, 1970, price 12s. (60 n.p.) $1.50 BN-2

Publications of the British-North American Committee are available from:

In Great Britain:
British-North American Research Association,
12 Upper Belgrave Street, London, S.W.1. Telephone: 01 235 1833

In the United States of America:
National Planning Association,
1606 New Hampshire Avenue, N.W., Washington, D.C. 20009
Telephone: 202-265-7685

In Canada:
Private Planning Association of Canada,
2060 Sun Life Building,
Montreal 110, Quebec. Telephone: 514-861-6319